TOYMAKING BASICS

David Wakefield

 Sterling Publishing Co., Inc. New York

Dedication

For Amy, my one and only.

Library of Congress Cataloging-in-Publication Data

Wakefield, David.
   Toymaking basics / by David Wakefield.
      p.   cm.
   Includes index.
   ISBN 0-8069-8750-2
   1. Wooden toy making—Amateurs' manuals.   I. Title.
TT174.5.W6W37   1993
745.592—dc20
                                  92-45043
                                    CIP

10 9 8 7 6 5 4 3 2 1

Published by Sterling Publishing Company, Inc.
387 Park Avenue South, New York, N.Y. 10016
© 1993 by David Wakefield
Distributed in Canada by Sterling Publishing
℅ Canadian Manda Group, P.O. Box 920, Station U
Toronto, Ontario, Canada M8Z 5P9
Distributed in Great Britain and Europe by Cassell PLC
Villiers House, 41/47 Strand, London WC2N 5JE, England
Distributed in Australia by Capricorn Link Ltd.
P.O. Box 665, Lane Cove, NSW 2066
Manufactured in the United States of America
All rights reserved

Sterling ISBN 0-8069-8750-2

Contents

INTRODUCTION

I have written *Toymaking Basics* in an attempt to open up the world of toymaking to everyone.

Toymaking is an easy craft to learn. With a few tools and an understanding of some simple techniques, you can get satisfactory results almost immediately.

I have made this book as straightforward as possible in hopes that anyone with an interest in toymaking will find it helpful. The book will more likely be found on the workbench, dog-eared and broken in, than on the coffee table.

Several projects are included in Chapter 10. I tried to design toys that cover a wide range, both in techniques and in types. They are worth making and provide a perfect opportunity to practise your skills on.

The information provided in the following pages will guide you through the basics of toymaking. This information is the key to learning a craft that will provide you with endless hours of enjoyment.

Sincerely,
David Wakefield

Chapter 1
MATERIALS

Toymaking can cover a huge range of projects, from a delicate infant's rattle to a durable outdoor swing. Because of this, the material needs are also quite varied. Following is information concerning the factors that will influence your choice of appropriate materials.

Hardwood versus Softwood

"Hardwood" refers to the wood from deciduous trees. "Softwood" refers to the wood from coniferous trees, trees with cones and needles (Illus. 1-1 and 1-2). The terms "deciduous" and "con-iferous" can be misleading because some conifers, such as larch and bald cypress, actually lose their needles in the winter, and many hardwoods in the tropics do not lose their leaves.

Chart 1-1 details some of the many differences between hardwoods and softwoods. Keep in mind that these are general characteristics. There is a lot of variation among the types of wood that fall within the categories hardwood and softwood. For example, some softwoods are hard and strong and some hardwoods are soft and weak. You don't want to make an infant toy out of softwood because it will splinter if a baby chews on it. Likewise, you wouldn't want to use softwood for a rocker, because it isn't strong enough to withstand

Illus. 1-1. Leaves from a deciduous tree.

Illus. 1-2. Cone and needles from a coniferous tree.

Chart 1-1. Some of the differences between hardwoods and softwoods.

Hardwood	Softwood
Leaves	Needles
Oak, maple, cherry, walnut	Pine, spruce, fir, cedar
Harder	Softer (Dents easily)
Heavy	Light
Stronger	Weaker
Sap (Not gummy)	Resin (Gums up blades and sandpaper)
Doesn't Tend to Splinter	Splinters Easily
Must Drill to Nail	Can Be Nailed
Expensive	Inexpensive

heavy use. Toy blocks could be made out of maple, but pine would work quite well as long as the edges were rounded to avoid splintering. They would be light, easy to play with, and 2 × 4 pine is so inexpensive that you can make quite an elaborate set for very little money (if you use construction scraps).

Both hardwood and softwood come in grades or numbers. Wood designated as #3 grade is about 50 percent knot-free, #2 is about 70 percent knot-free, and #1 is about 90 percent knot-free. "Clear," or "select," wood has one side totally knot-free. Wood that has not been graded is called "mill-run." It varies in quality.

For many types of toys, you can cut around knots or even include them in the toy, so you can save quite a bit of money by using low-grade, or mill-run, wood.

Sources of Softwood

Softwood is easily available at the local lumberyard. If there isn't one in your town, there's bound to be one nearby. Try the Yellow Pages under "Lumber." Lumberyards will always have a good selection of softwood, because it is used primarily in construction, and lumberyards are suppliers of the carpentry trade.

Softwood comes in standard thicknesses of 1, 2,

or 4 inches and widths from 2 to 12 inches (in 2-inch increments). Keep in mind that the boards have already been surfaced on all four sides and the actual dimensions are less than what they are called (Chart 1-2).

Nominal Size	Actual Size
1″ × 4″	¾″ × 3½″
1″ × 6″	¾″ × 5½″
1″ × 8″	¾″ × 7¼″
1″ × 10″	¾″ × 9¼″
1″ × 12″	¾″ × 11¼″
2″ × 4″	1½″ × 3½″
2″ × 6″	1½″ × 5½″
2″ × 8″	1½″ × 7¼″
2″ × 10″	1½″ × 9¼″
2″ × 12″	1½″ × 11¼″

Chart 1-2. Softwood at the lumberyard has already been surfaced on all four sides and its final dimensions are smaller than the rough dimensions given.

If you don't have either a table saw or a radial arm saw, lumberyards will, for a fee, usually rip or crosscut stock to the dimensions needed. For the resourceful, construction sites are a good place to find lots of small cut-off pieces of 2 × 4s. With a little tact, you can get quite a pile of scraps for free.

Sources of Hardwood

Lumberyards usually have a small selection of hardwood for trim, etc. Their prices are often very high because of the limited demand and the high grade of the wood, but toys use so little wood that this may be the best source for small quantities. However, remember that lower-grade wood is much cheaper and you can usually cut around knots (or even leave them) for toymaking.

Many woodworking supply companies that advertise in magazines sell hardwood. These woodworking magazines can usually be found at the local newsstand. Here again, the prices are usually pretty high, especially when you add the cost of shipping. Some catalogues, though, carry quite a selection of specialty woods. There are also many companies listed in these magazines that specialize in selling hardwood.

If you live in an area where hardwoods grow, there will probably be a hardwood lumberyard somewhere fairly near. This is the best source of kiln-dried wood. Because it's local, you avoid shipping costs. There will be a good variety of species to choose from, and you can select the size board that you want, as well as the quality. Most hardwood lumberyards will plane your wood to your specifications, for a reasonable fee. Again, keep in mind that lower-grade hardwood is much less expensive and will work quite nicely for most toys.

If you live in a heavily forested area, there may also be sawmills nearby. Try the state Department of Natural Resources, Division of Forestry, for their locations. Sawmills are an excellent source of inexpensive hardwood. You will, however, have to dry the wood before you use it.

There may also be some free sources of hardwood available. Motorcycle crates (especially Japanese) are quite often made of interesting hardwoods. Discarded pallets are usually made of hardwood. Old barns are also a great source of hardwood. I took down a barn that had walnut 10 × 10s for corner posts and cherry 2 × 6s for rafters. Make sure you remove all the nails before you start cutting into any recycled wood.

Drying Wood

There are two ways to dry green wood from the sawmill: air-drying and kiln-drying. Each has its advantages and disadvantages (Chart 1-3). Each method is described below.

Air-Drying

If you have the time and the space, air-drying wood can save much more money than buying kiln-dried wood. Most toys use such small pieces of wood that air-dried lumber will work just fine. Keep in mind that the spot you pick should have good air circulation so that the moisture in the

	Air-Drying	Kiln-Drying
Location	Attic: usually too hot and dry, wood cracks and warps Basement: too wet, wood rots Outside or in barn under the following circumstances: 1. air movement (fan or breeze); 2. it is not too hot; and 3. the wood is kept covered	As a kiln is a closed system, it can be set up anywhere. Operates like an oven but with control of humidity as well as temperature
Cost	Free	Usually increases cost by about $1.00/board foot
Time	About one year per inch thickness	From 20–90 days
Fuels	Air that's drier than the wood	Gas— most common Steam— from sawmill wood chips Solar— free but takes longer and is hard to control Elec.— dehumidification— extremely efficient and inexpensive
Results	Usually less stable—more likely to shrink, swell, and warp	Usually more stable—less likely to shrink, swell, and warp

Chart 1-3. Some of the most important differences between kiln-drying and air-drying.

wood can be carried away. Also, the boards have to be perfectly flat (and well up off the ground if outside). This may mean building a rack (see *How to Make Animated Toys,* by David Wakefield, for plans). The sticks between the rows should be ¾–1 inch wide and ¾–1 inch thick. If they are any wider (side to side), they will prevent the moisture from leaving the board under the sticks and the wood will rot in those areas. If they are any thinner (top to bottom), there won't be enough air circulation between the layers and the entire surfaces will suffer from mildew and rot instead of drying. The sticks should be made of kiln-dried wood to prevent moisture buildup between the sticks and the boards.

The sticks should also be placed directly over each other to provide continuous support. The boards should go all the way to the edge of the stacks so that no boards are left unsupported.

Wrapping the stacks with plastic would keep the weather out, but would also keep the wood's moisture in. A removable roof can be easily made of 2 × 2s and plastic. You'll have to replace the plastic every year or so, because it will deteriorate in the direct sun.

A moisture metre can be used to determine when the wood is dry enough to use (Illus. 1-3). (Moisture metres are available in most woodworking catalogues.) How much moisture your wood will ultimately have depends a great deal on the climate in your area. If the moisture content of the wood can be reduced to 8–10 percent, you have done a good job.

If your shop is dryer than 8–10 percent, bring the wood into your shop (on sticks) for two to four weeks to let it dry out a little more before you use it. To determine the moisture content of your shop, try the moisture metre on your workbench.

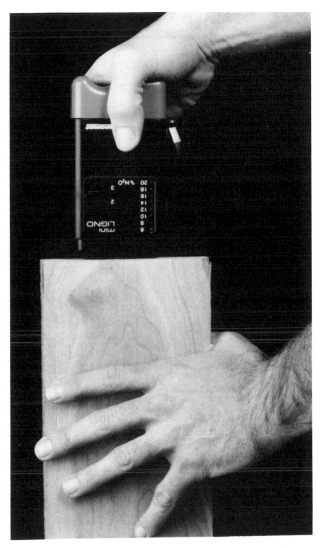

Illus. 1-3. Using a moisture metre to determine the moisture content of wood.

Kiln-Drying

Although some commercial gas-fired kilns will custom-dry wood for you, solar or electric kilns are the only kilns generally available. A solar kiln is difficult to control and can work slowly in areas with little sunshine. There are, however, plans available through the United States Department of Agriculture for building a workable solar kiln.

The electric kiln works on the same principle as a dehumidifier and is called a dehumidification kiln. The kilns are very compact and also quite inexpensive, both to purchase and to operate.

Unlike solar kilns, they have controls for both temperature and humidity, so the results are predictable and highly satisfactory.

There are two manufacturers of electric dehumidification kilns in the United States (Illus. 1-4). Both of these companies make a small (under 1,000 board feet) kiln suitable for the serious hobbyist or small business (Illus. 1-5). The money saved by drying your own wood will easily pay for the kiln in one or two loads.

Plywood

Some large toys are best built out of plywood. Plywood is extremely stable and strong and fairly

Illus. 1-4. The Nyle L-33 dehumidification wood dryer. It will be set inside an insulated plywood box that you build. The plywood box acts as the kiln. The kiln has baffles and a fan that move air through the wood, and then the dehumidifier. For more information on this and other wood dryers, write to Nyle Standard Dryers, Inc., P.O. Box 1107, Bangor, Maine 04402-1107.

Illus. 1-5. An insulated plywood kiln built to house the EBAC-LD 800 dehumidification wood dryer. Inside the kiln is the dryer and 800 board feet of 4/4 cherry. Note the external controls for the heater and the dehumidifier. The water is discharged by means of a hose at the bottom which can either be collected and emptied daily or run into a floor drain, etc., as shown here. For more information on this and other kilns, write to EBAC Lumber Dryers, 106 John Jefferson Road, Suite 102, Williamsburg, Virginia 23185.

inexpensive. There are several considerations to keep in mind when choosing the appropriate plywood (Chart 1-4).

Parts and Accessories for the Finished Toy

There are a whole host of dowels, pegs, wheels, etc., that are used in toymaking (Illus. 1-6). There are also a large number of suppliers. Woodworking magazines have advertisements for woodworking supply catalogues. Some catalogues will carry a greater variety of parts than others, and prices will also vary from one company to the next, so it might be helpful to write to several different stores for their catalogues.

Dowels can be found at most hardware stores. Once you've got your catalogues, compare the prices of dowels sold by different hardware stores to determine which are cheaper. Be aware, however, that dowels differ in quality. Some hardware stores carry dowels made from soft maple (red or silver maple) or soft Asian hardwoods. Use dowels

made from either birch or hard maple (sugar maple). If your thumbnail will cut deeply into the dowel, it's a soft hardwood (not birch or maple).

Though you can make your own wheels quite easily, manufactured wheels do have one advantage. They have a protruding hub around the axle hole. This makes it possible to machine-sand the axle ends (after gluing) without sanding the sur-

INTERIOR	EXTERIOR
Use water-soluble glue	Use waterproof glue
A-C grade is smooth and knot-free on one side, rough on the other	CDX—knotty and rough on both sides
3 PLY is inexpensive, there are holes or voids between the layers, and it can warp	Marine-grade is expensive, has five or more plies, and is very stable

Chart 1-4. Working characteristics of interior- and exterior-grade plywood.

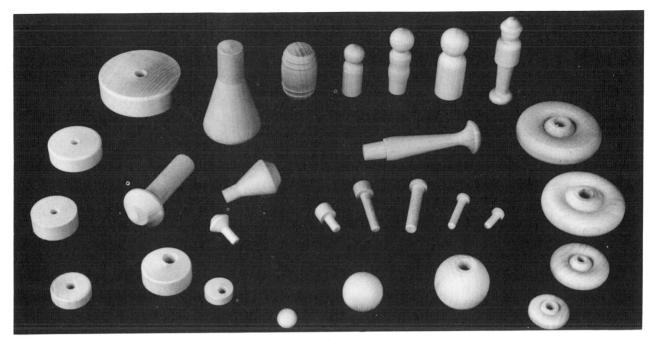

Illus. 1-6. *A few of the more common toy parts you can buy.*

Illus. 1-7. *Manufactured wheels have a protruding hub which you can sand (after the axle is glued in place) without having to sand the whole face of the wheel.*

face of the wheel (Illus. 1-7). If you make your own wheels, you'll have to sand the whole flat surface of the wheel to remove glue and the rough axle end.

Sandpaper

Grit

In toymaking, you will be sanding with sandpaper sheets and belts (Chart 1-5). Sandpaper sheets and belts come in many different grits. The higher the grit, the finer the abrasive material, and the smoother the finish.

In general, I use only two grits of sandpaper. I use #80-grit sheets to remove the marks left by the rasp, any burns or roughness left by the router, and even saw marks from the band saw in areas that the belt sander can't reach. I use #120-grit sheets to remove marks left by the file or the scratches left by #80-grit paper. For an infant toy like the rattle in Chapter 10, use a finer-grit paper such as #180 or #220 (or even finer) so that the toy feels smooth in the child's delicate hands.

On the belt sanders, I use #80-grit belts to remove any marks left by the thickness planers

SANDPAPER

	SHEETS	BELTS
Grits used in toymaking	Usually #80 and #120 Sometimes #220 or finer	Usually #80 and #120
Backing material	*Paper* holds up adequately *Cloth*, wet-and-dry, lasts a long time	*Paper* wears out quickly *Cloth* holds up
Materials	*Garnet, flint,* and *aluminum oxide* are all okay	*Aluminum oxide* is good for wood; *silicone carbide* should be used between coats of hard finish; *zinc oxide* should be used for metal
Bonding	*Glue*, which forms a good bond	*Glue* dissolves and weakens; *resin* lasts much longer
Coating	*Open coats* load up *Closed coats* do not load up as much	*Uncoated belts* load up and won't clean well; *resin-coated belts* don't load up as badly, clean easily, and last much longer

Chart 1-5. Different sandpaper sheets are available for different jobs. Sanding belts, however, should be made of X-weight cloth with resin-bonded and resin-coated abrasive.

and saw marks left by the band saw, from cutting out the silhouettes or resawing. Then I use #120-grit belts to remove the scratches left by the #80-grit belts both with the grain (on the surfaces) and across the grain (on the edges).

Backing Material

Sandpaper sheets are generally made of paper, although wet-and-dry sandpaper is often made of cloth. The cloth will hold up longer, but is not as flexible and is more expensive. Wet-or-dry sandpaper works well for sanding between coats of hard finish (because the water keeps the finish from clogging the surface of the paper) and for applying oil finishes (while removing the grain that is raised up by the oil).

Sanding belts are available in both paper and cloth. Use cloth belts, because they will last much longer than paper.

Weight and Flexibility

Sandpaper sheets usually come in either "A" or "C" weight. "A" weight sheets are thinner and more flexible, but break down quickly, while "C" weight sheets are thicker, stiffer, and last longer.

Belts usually come in either "X" or "J" weight. "J" weight belts are more flexible, but "X" weight belts are tougher and will last longer.

Abrasive Material

Traditional abrasives include natural abrasives like flint and garnet. Many woodworkers still prefer these. There are also two synthetics that are used now: aluminum oxide, which is great for sanding wood, and silicon carbide, which is good for sanding between coats of a hard finish such as varnish or polyurethane. Try all these abrasive materials, compare prices, and determine which you prefer. The abrasive material isn't nearly as important as the backing, the bonding agent, and the coating.

Bonding

The abrasive material on sheets is usually bonded with glue. In the case of wet-or-dry sandpaper, waterproof glue is used.

Belts, however, use different bonding materials. When glue is used on belts, the heat of friction usually breaks down the glue before the particles are worn out. For this reason, resin is now used to bond the particles to the backing. It lasts much longer and many hardware stores now stock resin-bonded belts. Woodworking catalogues also advertise resin-bonded belts.

Coating

With belts, a coating of resin stops the abrasive particles from clogging up with sawdust, makes the abrasive last longer, and makes the belt easier to clean (with a belt cleaner). Again, this makes a great deal of difference. **Be sure to get resin-bonded and -coated cloth belts.**

Belt Cleaner

A belt cleaner is indispensable for toymaking. It pulls the dust particles off the belt and unclogs the abrasive. It can make your belts last much longer, and, of course, the belt cuts better too when it's clean (Illus. 1-8).

Glue

For toys that will not be exposed to the weather, aliphatic resin is the best glue to use. Aliphatic resin is the white or yellow glue that can be found in hardware stores. Yellow glue is stronger, and can also be found in any woodworking catalogue. Aliphatic resin glue must be clamped, when it is drying, to work properly. But once it has set up, it is stronger than the wood that it joins.

Use a waterproof glue on outdoor toys such as the Animal Glider in Chapter 10. Resorcinol used to be the only waterproof glue available. It has to be mixed before use and is black in color, making it unattractive for toys. Franklin Adhesives has come out with a waterproof glue called Titebond II®. It is a one-part glue that dries clear and is water-soluble before drying, which makes it a lot easier to work with.

Finishes

Special consideration should be given to the finishes for two types of toys: infant toys and outdoor toys. Each is described below.

Infant Toys

Infants will put anything in their mouths. This means that any toys made for infants will have to be finished with nontoxic products. Mineral oil will work quite well, but over time it will evaporate and the toy will need to be reoiled, or the wood will dry out. You can find mineral oil at the drugstore.

There are several resin oils that polymerize, or harden, as they dry. They fill the wood up to the surface without forming a hard coating over the wood. The wood keeps its natural appearance but has some protection from dirt, water, and abrasion. Some of these finishes are nontoxic when used directly from the can, while some of them

Illus. 1-8. If you use a belt cleaner regularly, your belts will last much longer.

need 30 days' drying to become nontoxic. Look for them in woodworking catalogues or hardware stores.

There are also nontoxic dyes available in bright colors for infants', toddlers', and children's toys.

Outdoor Toys

Outdoor toys can be protected in several ways. The easiest finish is a stain with a base coat of mineral spirits. If you choose a relatively rot-resistant wood, such as white oak, catalpa, locust, mahogany, osage orange, teak, redwood, or cedar, the stain will give it added rot resistance and also prevent it from turning grey. Stain is available in paint stores.

Oil or latex paint can give your toy a hard and colorful protective coat. Be sure to use a good primer first. Coat all areas, to prevent the weather from entering them.

There are many clear, hard waterproof finishes. Varnish and lacquer were the standards for years before synthetics. Polyurethane (a synthetic) is the toughest, longest-lasting hard clear finish available. All three of these finishes can be found at hardware stores.

Chapter 2
TOYMAKING OPERATIONS AND TOOLS

There are many ways to approach toymaking. But, whether you are making one simple softwood silhouette with wheels or going into production of sculpted hardwood rockers, there are certain operations common to all types of toymaking that will require hand or power tools. In most cases,

Illus. 2-1. A few basic tools can get you started as a toymaker.

Illus. 2-2. The well-equipped shop makes toymaking easier and will also increase the efficiency and productivity of the professional toymaker.

you will only need a few inexpensive tools if you are willing to spend more time and effort making the toys (Illus. 2-1 and 2-2).

Toymaking can be broken down into six basic operations: planing, cutting, drilling, sanding, rounding edges, and gluing. Certain tools are needed for each of these operations. Following is an overview of each of these areas that describes the advantages and disadvantages of using different tools.

Planing

The thickness planer is used to plane wood. It is potentially the most expensive tool in your shop. It is also the least needed tool in the workshop.

This is because if you buy softwood from the lumberyard, it will be planed already, on both the surface and the edges. If you buy hardwood from a mail-order company or a regular lumberyard, it will be planed already. Also, most hardwood lumberyards will have a thickness planer and will plane your wood for you (for a fee).

If you are buying your lumber rough, there is one more option, besides buying a thickness planer. Most vocational schools will have a thickness planer. Quite often they will plane wood for you, at a reasonable price, as part of their classes.

A thickness planer, however, can be an extremely useful tool to have for toymaking. There are many toys that are best made with boards that are not the standard thicknesses that are available. You may want a board that is ½ inch thick instead of the standard ¾ or ¹³⁄₁₆ inch.

Fortunately, you do not have to buy a $5,000 thickness planer to do your own planing. There are many 10–12-inch thickness planers now on the market that will do a fine job of planing small quantities of wood. Some cost as little as $400. The blades on these small planers run at a high rpm (revolutions per minute) with little horsepower. This means that they have the power to only plane off ¹⁄₃₂ inch at a pass instead of ⅛ inch, and boards cannot be fed through them very quickly. These planers, however, will give you an extremely smooth surface, if you keep the blades sharp. This can save you some time when sanding.

You can make a simple stand (for these portable planers) that will support the planer at a comfortable height and will also enable you to feed a fairly long board through by yourself (Illus. 2-3).

Cutting

In toymaking, as opposed to other areas of woodworking, a jointer, table saw, or radial arm saw are not essential. These tools can be used for some toys, such as blocks, but blocks can be made just as easily without them. For this reason, these tools are not described in this book. Below is a description of six tools that can be used for cutting: the band saw, the scroll saw (jigsaw), the portable electric jigsaw, the coping saw, the backsaw, and the flexible handsaw.

Band Saw

The toymaker needs a tool that will cut curved lines. The band saw is the best tool for this job. It will cut curves more quickly than any other tool, especially in thick hardwood. Because the band saw has a continuous band that cuts in one direction, the teeth are always cutting. The spinning wheels and the large motor (usually ¾ horsepower or more) prevent the band saw from binding up in thick, hard material.

Remember that a band saw can be set up with a very wide blade for resawing and a very narrow blade (⅛ inch) for extremely tight curves, as well as sizes in between for normal curved cutting.

Use a band saw with a tilting table to make compound cuts like the curved cuts made at an angle for rockers (Illus. 2-4).

The two-wheel 14-inch band saw is probably the best all-around band saw. Band saws are available in a wide range of prices. The cost of the band saw will reflect its quality.

The band saw is the most important tool for

Illus. 2-3. A simple stand can be made with 2 × 4's and drywall screws, to raise the planer up to worker height. The out-feed side will help the sole operator.

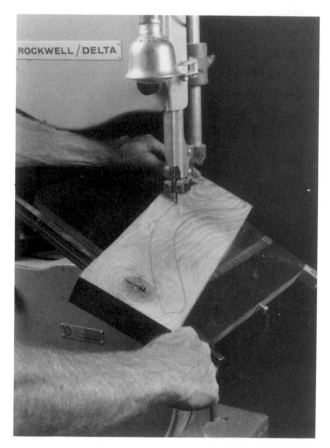

Illus. 2-4. The tilting table on the band saw enables you to cut compound angles (curved cuts with a bevel).

toymaking. If you plan to make many toys, your very first power tool should be a band saw.

Scroll Saw

The scroll saw or jigsaw is helpful for toymaking. It is especially useful for thin softwood cutouts, fine work (jigsaw puzzles), and inside cuts that can't be made with the band saw (Illus. 2-5).

Because the blade moves up and down, even a small machine has very deep throat (distance from arm to blade). The blades are cheaper than band saw blades and you can get *extremely* fine blades as well.

The scroll saw is, however, quite limited. Because the blades move up and down, they are only cutting half the time. The teeth are generally so small that the sawdust is not cleared away as efficiently. Scroll saw blades just don't cut that quickly. They also have a very hard time with thick or hard material and will not resaw boards.

If you are going to do a lot of extremely fine work, the scroll saw is the tool to use. For general toymaking, use a band saw, because it is much faster and more versatile.

Portable Electric Jigsaw

The jigsaw is quite an inexpensive but handy tool. It is perfect for large, irregular shapes (plywood) that are too big for the band saw (Illus. 2-6). If your

Illus. 2-5. Because the blade on a scroll saw can be removed and fed through the work, it can cut inside curves.

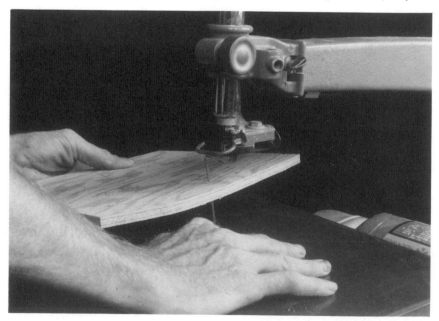

Illus. 2-6. The portable jigsaw is great for curved cuts, or for cutting pieces that are too large for the band saw or scroll saw.

jigsaw is powerful enough (and you have a large enough blade), you can cut through fairly thick material.

The blade on a jigsaw has no guides or tension to keep it straight, so it tends to bend to the sides. Going slowly will help to prevent this somewhat.

Coping Saw

The inexpensive coping saw can be used to cut out silhouettes, though it is a tedious, time-consuming process. You can, however, get satisfactory results if you transfer your pattern to both sides of the wood and cut carefully, following both silhouettes (Illus 2-7).

Backsaw (Dovetail Saw) and Flexible Handsaw

A backsaw has a piece of steel folded over its back to keep it rigid (Illus. 2-8). In toymaking, the cuts are generally so small and simple that the blade does not need to be rigid for accuracy, as it does in a dovetail joint. If you have this type of saw already, however, it will cut just fine.

A flexible saw has no back on it, so it can flex. The real advantage to this type of saw when used for toymaking is that it will cut the end of a protruding dowel without scratching the surface of the rest of the toy (Illus. 2-9). My saw is handmade, but Japanese versions of this saw are available in many woodworking catalogues.

Drilling

Drilling holes is an essential part of toymaking. Many of the holes in toymaking are for axles, peg holes, etc., so they must be perpendicular to the wood's surface. This requires a drill press. If you don't have a standard drill press (bench or floor model), you can use one of several available de-

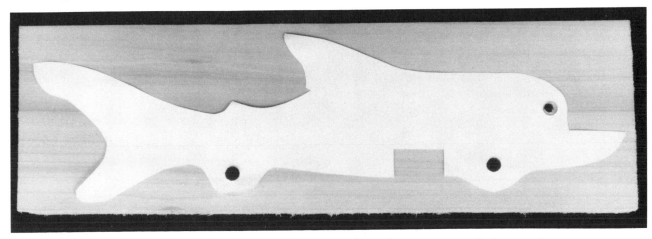

Illus. 2-7. After you lay out your pattern, drill the holes, and use them to accurately lay out the pattern on the reverse side. Then follow both silhouettes with the coping saw. This is not an easy process, but it can be done if there is no alternative.

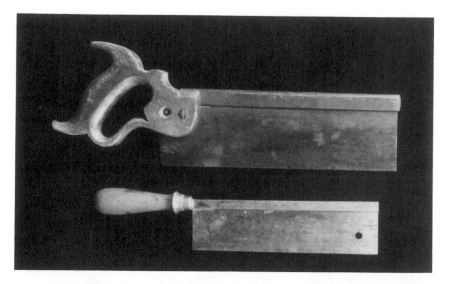

Illus. 2-8. The backsaw has a steel support down its back, to prevent it from flexing.

Illus. 2-9. A flexible saw will enable you to saw dowels, etc., flush to your work without tearing up the surface.

vices that hold a portable electric drill perpendicular to the work (Illus. 2-10). They will also help you drill into dowels, and some can be set at different angles.

Sanding

As soon as you make your first toy, you'll find out that about half of the work that goes into a quality toy is sanding. There are two basic sanding operations: sanding the flat surfaces (with the grain) and sanding the edges, or silhouette (across the grain). Quite a bit of hard sanding is also involved, but because no tools are *required* for this technique it is described in Chapter 7.

Sanding Flat Surfaces

A belt sander is essential for sanding flat surfaces. Ideally, you'll have a stationary belt sander (6 × 48 inches) for sanding small pieces (blocks, rolling toys, etc.) (Illus. 2-11) and a portable belt sander (4 × 24 inches or 3 × 23½ inches) for large pieces like those used on a swing (Illus. 2-12).

If you don't have both belt sanders, you can convert your portable belt sander to a stationary one by clamping it upside down in the vise (Illus.

Illus. 2-10. *A portable drill can be outfitted to drill holes that are perpendicular to the surface of the toy part.*

Illus. 2-11. *A 6 × 48-inch stationary belt sander is the ideal tool for sanding flat surfaces.*

2-13). It's a little smaller than a stationary 6 × 48-inch belt sander, but it can be used on most of the toy projects described in Chapter 10.

Of course, you can use a block of wood and sandpaper to hand-sand the flat surfaces, especially if they're planed smoothly.

Sanding Edges, or Silhouettes

The edges can also be sanded by hand, with the help of sanding blocks (Illus. 2-14), but I highly recommend getting a 1-inch sander-grinder (Illus. 2-15). They are quite inexpensive and will make short work out of an otherwise tedious task.

Illus. 2-12 (left). *A portable belt sander is needed for the flat surfaces of parts that are too large to sand on the stationary belt sander.*

Illus. 2-13. *You can convert your portable belt sander into a stationary one by securely clamping it, upside down, in a vise.*

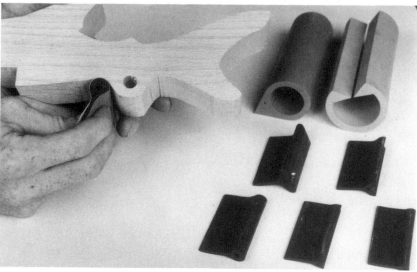

Illus. 2-14. *The edges of a silhouette can be sanded by hand, with the help of curved sanding blocks.*

Rounding Edges

Toys are made to be *handled*, mostly by children. So all the corners and edges need to be smooth. Some of the smaller pieces can simply be rounded over slightly with sandpaper, but the edges on most large pieces have to be rounded over quite a bit so the pieces feel good when played with and so children won't get splinters (Illus. 2-16).

The router, with a carbide-tipped quarter-round bit, is the perfect tool for the job. It is also a

Illus. 2-15 (left). *The 1-inch sander (edge sander) is essential for the serious toymaker.*

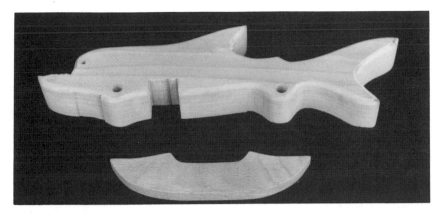

Illus. 2-16. You can hand-sand the corners of small pieces to break their sharp edges. Larger pieces should be thoroughly sanded over.

potentially dangerous tool. Be very careful when using a router. If you are not experienced, do not attempt to round the edges of small toy parts with the router (see Chapter 7 for more detail on rounding edges).

Another excellent tool that will do the same job as the router is the four-in-hand. A four-in-hand is a combination flat-and-curved rasp and flat-and-curved file. The rasp will cut away material very quickly, and the file will smooth the rasp marks enough to they can be hand-sanded with #80 and #120 sandpaper (Illus. 2-17).

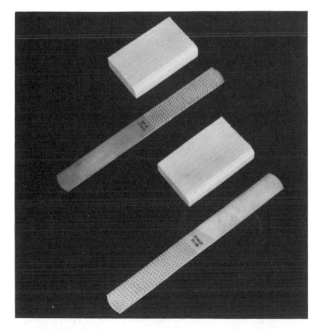

Illus. 2-17. The 8-inch four-in-hand is the perfect tool for thoroughly rounding edges. The rasp does the cutting and the file smooths the rasp marks enough so you can hand-sand them.

Gluing

Two general types of tools are needed for gluing: glue applicators and clamps. Each is described below.

Glue Applicators

When gluing boards together, you can spread the glue with your finger or a cheap brush (Illus. 2-18 and 2-19). Glue can be applied to axle holes and peg holes, etc., with the wide end of a flat toothpick (Illus. 2-20).

There are applicators available that make gluing neater or more efficient (Illus. 2-21 and 2-22).

Illus. 2-18. Glue can be spread with your fingers.

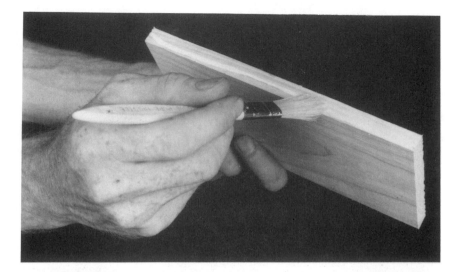

Illus. **2-19.** *A cheap brush is a good way to spread glue.*

Illus. **2-20.** *A toothpick can be used to spread glue on the inside walls of a hole.*

Illus. **2-21.** *There are several applicators that will neatly spread glue on flat joints.*

Illus. **2-22.** *There are several applicators available for putting glue on the insides of holes. They speed up production work.*

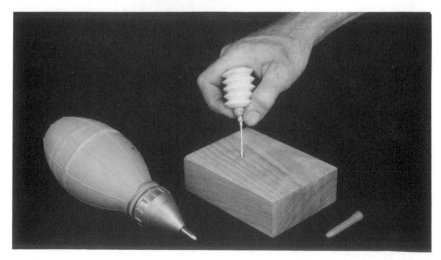

Clamps

In toymaking, you will generally be using aliphatic resin glue, and the wood will have to be clamped while the glue sets up. There are many types of clamps available today (Illus. 2-23), but you can make most toys with two or three bar clamps and four C-clamps (Illus. 2-24). You can easily add one or two clamps at a time as your shop grows.

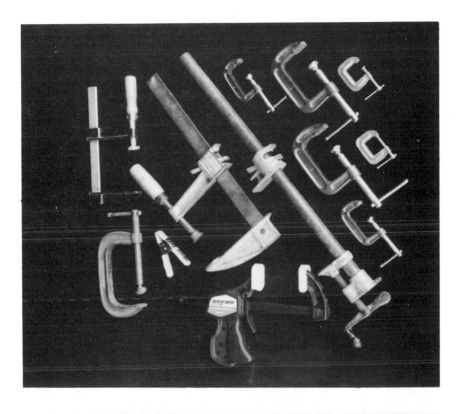

Illus. 2-23. A wide variety of clamps are available today.

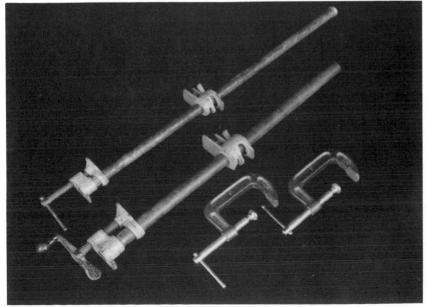

Illus. 2-24. Just a few C-clamps and bar clamps are needed to get started in toymaking.

Chapter 3
SAFETY TECHNIQUES

In toymaking, as in any other type of woodworking, safety should be a top priority. Chapter 5 has safety instructions for specific power tools. Follow these instructions carefully. Below are general safety guidelines. Incorporate these guidelines in your woodworking routine.

1. Wear the proper safety equipment when woodworking. Wear eye protection because there is always the possibility that cut material or sawdust may fly into your eyes. It is best to use safety glasses that are AINSI approved. (The lettering AINSI will be stamped on them.) They should have side shields that protect your eyes from the side as well as the front. If you wear prescription glasses, goggles will fit over them and protect your eyes from the sides.

A good, close-fitting dust mask is also essential. The long-term effects of inhaling wood dust can be quite harmful, especially if you are using woods that are irritating to the sinuses or toxic.

Also wear ear protection. Operating high-decibel equipment like a router or thickness planer without ear protection over a long period of time will result in hearing loss. It is a good idea to try different ear protection until you find the type that you are comfortable with, so that you will find it easier to develop the habit of using it.

2. Make sure that your shirt is tucked in at the waist and your shirt sleeves are rolled up past your elbows. This is a simple precaution that will prevent clothing from getting caught by spinning blades and bits and yanking you into the cutting surface. For the same reasons, remove any jewelry before working with power tools and tie long hair back.

3. Read the instructions that come with your tools and follow the manufacturer's safety and operating recommendations.

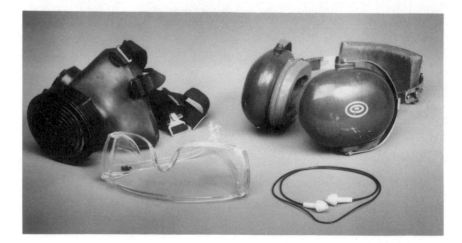

Illus. 3-1. Wear eye and ear protection and a dust mask when woodworking.

4. Use all safety equipment on the tools. Use the guards that come with the tools. Use push sticks to keep your hands well away from the cutting edge of power equipment.

5. Never work when you are under the influence of drugs or alcohol. Even over-the-counter and prescription drugs can cause drowsiness or other effects that would make it dangerous to use tools.

6. Keep your mind on your work and avoid distractions. Think through each procedure before doing it. Don't do it if you feel it is dangerous.

Chapter 4
PATTERNS

If you are making a small toy such as a rattle or a pull toy, the patterns are usually small enough to fit on the page of a book or a pattern sheet (at full size), so you can simply transfer them to your wood and start cutting (see "Transferring Patterns," pages 30 and 31). Quite often, though, the pattern is too large and must be reduced to fit on the page. So the first step is to enlarge the pattern to its actual size. Following are methods of enlarging patterns.

Enlarging Patterns

Enlarging Patterns with the Photocopier

The easiest way to enlarge patterns is on a photocopier (look in the Yellow Pages under "Copies").

If the patterns you have do not give you an exact percentage of enlargement on the photocopier, you can experiment until you end up with the correct dimensions (Illus. 4-1).

Most duplicating businesses have a photocopier that takes 11×17-inch paper, which is a pretty good-sized pattern. If the enlarged pattern is larger than the paper size of the machine, you can enlarge sections of the pattern and then join them together with clear tape. Before enlarging the sections, make lines on the pattern that will mark the exact intersection of the enlarged pieces. This way, they can be joined together accurately (Illus. 4-2).

Once the pieces are joined together, you can simply use this pattern the way it is (put tape on the back of the seams as well). Or, if you want a pattern that's easier to work with, you can run the whole assembly through an oversize duplicator (3-

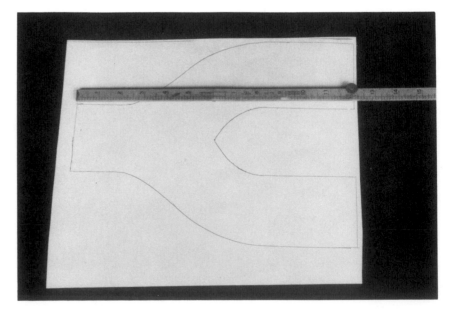

Illus. 4-1. If you know the dimensions of the finished pattern, you can experiment with the percentage of the enlargement until your pattern has the dimensions called for.

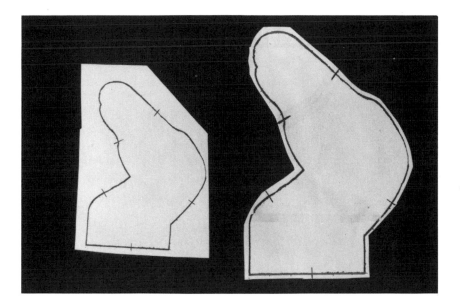

Illus. 4-2. If you make marks on your original (shown on the left), you can use them to accurately join your enlarged segments.

foot-wide duplicators are available, but they will not enlarge copies).

Enlarging Patterns with a Grid

Enlarging with a grid is the best way to enlarge *very* big patterns. If the pattern has a gridwork on it already, it will indicate what size these squares should be blown up to to enlarge to full-size. Draw a gridwork on a piece of paper with squares of the enlarged size. Then transfer points of line intersection from the small grid to the large one. This will give you a series of dots that can be joined by a French curve or a flexible tool (Illus. 4-3). Both of these tools will be available at an art store, college bookstore, or a drafting supply store. If you're going to do a lot of enlarging in this manner, you can draw one enlarged grid and use it over and over by laying tracing paper over it to mark the dots to join for your patterns (Illus. 4-3).

If your pattern doesn't have a grid on it, you'll have to draw one. Your grid will have to be the proper size. If the pattern in the book is 5 inches wide and needs to end up 20 inches wide, your finished grid will need to be four times the size of

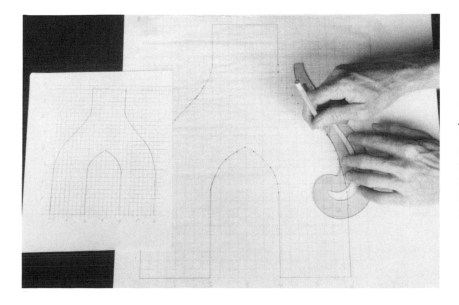

Illus. 4-3. Once you've transferred the dots in the grid system, you can join them together using a French curve or a flexible tool. You can use one grid for many enlargements by laying tracing paper over it to transfer the dots onto.

the grid you draw over the pattern. Therefore, you can draw ½-inch squares over a side of the original grid, and the final grid will have squares that are 2 inches on a side, or ¼-inch squares on the original and 1-inch squares on the final drawing if you want a finer grid (one with more points of intersection, and more accurate detail).

Enlarging Patterns with an Opaque Projector

Patterns can also be enlarged by an opaque projector. Simply project the pattern (lying flat on the projector) onto a wall with the paper taped up. Move the projector in and out until the image on the wall is the proper size, focus the image, and then draw the image onto the paper.

Transferring Patterns

Before transferring patterns from a book, you may want to photocopy them so that you don't have to tear the pages out of the book. Be sure the page is flat on the copier to avoid any distortion.

There are two basic ways to transfer patterns from a book: cutting them out and taping them to the wood or tracing them onto the wood. Both methods are described below.

Cutting Out and Taping Patterns

The quickest way to transfer patterns onto your wood is also a very accurate method. Cut out the pattern with scissors, leaving ¹⁄₁₆ to ⅛ inch around the edges. Do not cut right to the line. It takes longer because you have to be more careful, and there is the possibility that you will cut through the line, removing part of the accurate outline.

Tape the pattern to your wood. Sometimes a few well-placed pieces of tape will hold the pattern quite well (Illus. 4-4). Other times, you may need more tape (Illus 4-5). Make sure that the wood is free of dust or the tape won't stick.

Next, mark any hole locations so that you will drill them accurately after the silhouette is cut out and the pattern is no longer stuck to your wood. Use a hammer to tap a punch or a nail to mark the hole locations. Don't drill through the pattern or it may catch on the bit and get torn up (Illus. 4-6).

When you cut out the piece on the band saw or scroll saw, start with the tricky areas first while the pattern is still firmly attached to the wood, because the pattern will become gradually detached as you cut it out.

For very large, or complicated, pieces you may have to retape the pattern to the wood in a few places as you cut the piece out, to keep it from moving around (Illus. 4-7).

If you carefully saw the lines of the pattern without removing them, you will get a very accurate finished piece and you can use the pattern over again.

The one disadvantage to this method is that you have to drill the holes after the piece is cut out. Any holes near the edge of the piece will have to be drilled quite slowly and carefully to prevent the wood's splitting.

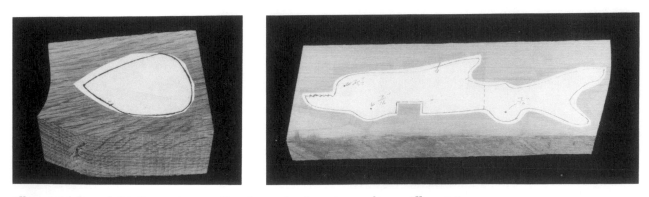

Illus. 4-4 (above left). Some pieces will only need a few pieces of tape. Illus. 4-5 (above right). Some pieces will need a lot of tape to hold them securely to your wood.

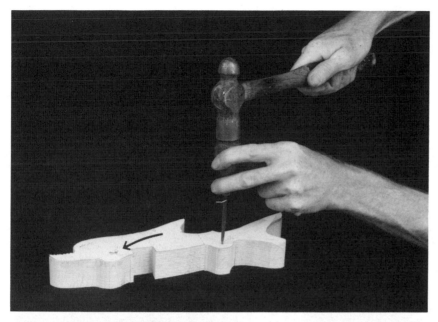

Illus. 4-6. Use a punch or a nail to transfer the hole locations accurately onto your work. Drilling through the pattern will tear it up. Note the torn front wheel hole.

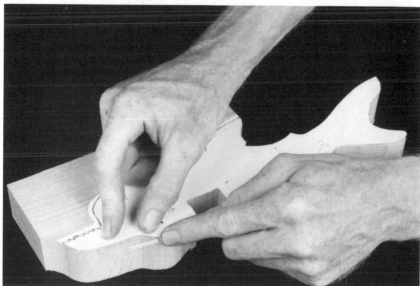

Illus. 4-7. Sometimes you'll need to retape the cut areas to your work so the pattern won't move.

Tracing Patterns

Tracing patterns works quite well on simple outlines like the shark toy in Chapter 10. Note that the hole locations of the shark, shown in Illus. 4-8, are marked with an X to help make drilling accurate.

Graphite paper is an excellent tracing paper. It transfers the drawing in pencil instead of ink. This way, you can erase your tracing lines after the piece is cut out. Graphite paper is available through some woodworking and toy part catalogues. It can also be found at drafting and art supply stores. Remember, white graphite paper will show up better on dark wood.

Hardboard Patterns

You may decide to make several of the same types of toy. In such a case, the best permanent pattern material to use for medium-sized toys is tempered hardboard. Use one of the above methods to

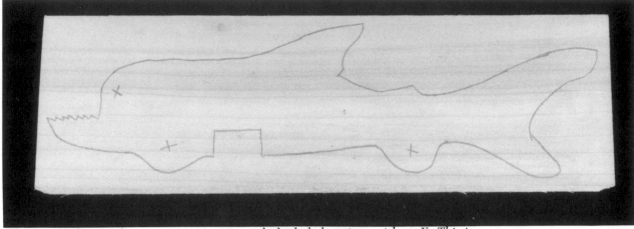

Illus. 4-8. *When you're tracing patterns, mark the hole locations with an X. This is easier to see than a dot and will also help you to be accurate when you are drilling.*

Illus. 4-9. *The holes in your patterns that are used to mark hole locations should be just large enough so that they form a small circle when you trace around them with a pencil.*

Illus. 4-10. *If the pattern has cuts that extend into the piece, the cut in the pattern will have to be wide enough to fit the tip of a pencil.*

transfer the paper pattern to the Masonite. When you drill the holes, don't drill them to their actual size. Instead, drill the hole locations with a ⅛-inch bit. This way, the hole will be just large enough to make a good circle when you draw around it with a pencil (Illus. 4-9).

Any lines that cut into the piece (not just a silhouette) will have to be widened enough to fit a pencil in the crack to mark the line (Illus. 4-10).

Rubber Stamps

If you are going to make a series of one small toy or toy part, use rubber stamps. They will save you a lot of time, especially with complicated patterns. Office supply stores can have rubber stamps made for you. Another option is to find the company that makes rubber stamps and have a sheet made with all the stamps you need. Then you can cut the pieces out, glue them to a piece of wood with contact cement, and cut them out on the band saw. I went so far as to put handles on my rubber stamps and assemble them in sets for each toy (Illus. 4-11).

The office supply store will also carry the ink pads that you'll need. You can pick a color that shows up well on the wood that you're using.

Illus. 4-11. As a production toy-maker, I even put little handles on my stamps and assembled them in sets, one set for each toy.

Chapter 5

CUTTING TOOLS AND TECHNIQUES

There are several tools used for sawing (or cutting) in toymaking. Below is a description of each of them that covers the general operating techniques, as well as some techniques specific to toymaking.

Band Saw

Setting Up the Band Saw

Before information is given on specific cutting techniques, it is important that woodworkers know how to set a band saw up properly.

When changing blades, either pull out the plug or shut off the breaker if it's wired directly. Next, remove the pin in the table slot, the insert, and the side covers (Illus. 5-1). Move all the guides back, above and below the table. They need to be totally out of the way so that they don't interfere with the blade's position when it is being set up.

First, adjust the tension. This is controlled by raising and lowering the upper wheel. Lower the upper wheel enough to slip the blade on (with the teeth facing down and forward).

Raise the upper wheel enough to hold the blade in place and rotate the upper wheel slowly by hand, to determine that the blade is not going to slip off. Then raise the upper wheel until the gauge indicates the width of the blade. The wider the blade, the more tension is applied (Illus. 5-2).

Once the tension is set up, you need to get the

Illus. 5-1. To change blades, turn off the power at its source and remove the side covers, the insert, and the pin. Move all the guides back so that they won't interfere with the new blade's "tracking."

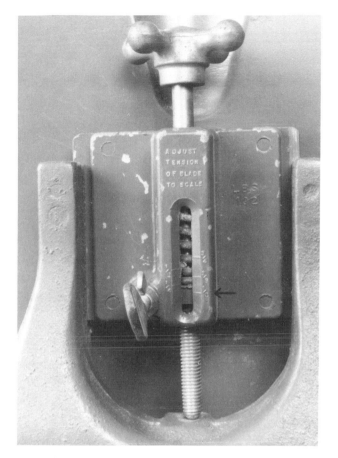

Illus. 5-2. The tension is set according to the width of the blade. The wider the blade, the more tension is applied. As the tension is increased, the spring is compressed and the indicator (at the base of the spring) moves up the scale (indicating the width of the blade in fractions of an inch).

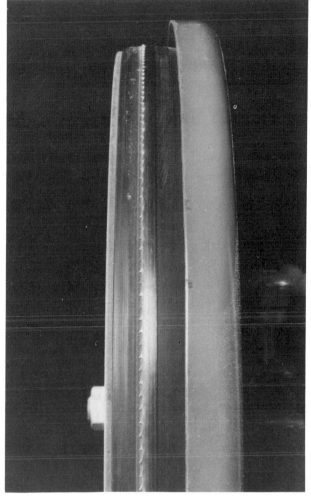

Illus. 5-3. The blade should track in the center of the tire (without the guides interfering).

blade "tracking" properly. The blade should run right in the center of the wheel's edge (Illus. 5-3). The upper wheel can be tilted to adjust where the blade tracks on the wheels. Turn the wheels by hand (in the direction they would run if you were sawing) and use the bolt to tilt the wheel back and forth until the blade runs right in the center of the "tire" (the rubber on the edge of the wheels). Be sure to lock the wheel in place after you've adjusted the tracking.

Now, the guides need to be positioned. Most guides have a roller bearing (or thrust bearing) behind the blade, to support the blade as wood is pushed against it. These bearings should be set first. They should not be touching the blade until wood is pushed against it. This minimizes the friction between the bearing and the blade. It also prevents the bearing from interfering with the blade's "tracking." So bring the upper thrust bearing up behind the blade, until there's about 1/16 inch between the bearing and the blade (Illus. 5-4). You should be able to see daylight between the thrust bearing and the back of the blade. If you push against the blade (when it's unplugged), it should easily move against the bearing and move away when you remove your finger. Repeat this same process for the thrust bearing under the table.

Next, adjust the side guides. There are three types of side guides: metal blocks, which will heat

Illus. 5-4. When the guides are set properly, you should be able to see daylight between the thrust bearing and the back of the blade.

Illus. 5-5. The side blocks (or rollers) are positioned as close to the blade as they can be without actually rubbing against it. (Make sure the weld in the blade doesn't hit the side blocks as it goes through.)

TOP VIEW OF BLADE BETWEEN BLOCKS

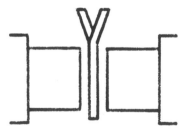

Illus. 5-6. The blocks (or rollers) should be as far forward as possible without taking the set out of the blade.

up and wear both themselves and the blade if the blade rubs against them; rollers, which will spin freely if the blade rubs against them; and blocks made of a composite material that can be pressed right against small blades that are hard to guide otherwise. When these blocks are used, the blade is held securely, but no heat is generated to wear the blade out prematurely.

Metal blocks and rollers are set up the same way. There are two adjustment steps:

1. The blocks (or rollers) should be as close as possible on either side of the blade without touching it (Illus 5-5). Band-saw blades are put together with a weld. If the weld is not perfect, there may be a slight bulge or kink. So it's a good idea to run the blade (rotate the upper wheel) all the way around to make sure that the weld does not hit the guides as it passes between them. Make sure that the guides are not pushing the blade to one side or the other, and that it is moving freely.

2. The guides should be as far forward as possible without interfering with the "set" (Illus. 5-6). Set is the amount the teeth are bent to either side—to give the rest of the blade free travel through the wood without friction. Remember that the blade will move back slightly until it hits the rear thrust bearing. So press the blade (with the band saw unplugged) against the rear roller bearing as you fine-tune the side guides' forward position. Repeat the process for the lower side guides.

Now you have all the guides set so that there is

the least possible friction to wear out the blade and guides.

Once the tension, tracking, and guides are adjusted, put the insert and the pin back in, replace the side covers, and plug the band saw back in.

The upper guides should be just above your work. This will help to keep your hands away from the blade. Also, the lower the top guides are, the more support the blade has.

As you raise and lower the top guide assembly to cut different thicknesses of wood, make sure that the guides line up properly with the blade as you tighten the guide assembly in its new position. It is very easy to let the assembly shift to either side so that one block is actually pushing the blade to the side (Illus. 5-7).

Once the guides are set, use a square to make sure that the worktable is at right angles to the blade.

Illus. 5-7. *If you're not careful, you can clamp the guide assembly off-center when you reposition it. This will cause one block to rub against the blade, and you can even push the blade to the side.*

Resawing

Toymaking requires many different thicknesses of wood. Sometimes wood can be planed to thickness, but quite often this would waste a lot of material. Hardwood is generally available in two thicknesses: 1 inch (4/4, or four-quarter) and 2 inches (8/4, or eight-quarter). If you need a board 3/8 inch thick, planing a rough 1-inch board to 3/8 inch would be quite wasteful. But if you resaw a 1-inch-

thick board, you should be able to get boards 3/8 inch thick by the time you plane them down. Resawing is the process of cutting a board in half along its width.

A resawing fence will help you to do an accurate job of resawing. Some band saws have a rip fence available as an accessory. They will work quite well for boards up to about 3 inches wide. For wider boards use a slightly taller fence for better support. Simply glue and screw two boards together on edge, at right angles to each other. A couple of braces cut at 90 degrees and screwed to the jig will make it more reliable (Illus 5-8).

When you clamp this jig to the band-saw table, make sure that it is parallel to the blade. Measure

Illus. 5-8. *A rip fence is easy to make. Glue and screw two straight boards together at right angles. Braces cut at 90 degrees can be fastened to the fence to make it more reliable.*

the distance from the mitre slot to the jig (at both ends of the table) (Illus. 5-9).

When you resaw wood, internal stresses may be released. This can cause the two resawed ends of the board to push together after they pass by the blade. This slot between the two halves of the board, called the kerf, can be kept open by slipping a little wedge of wood between the two pieces after they pass the blade (Illus. 5-10).

When you are using the band saw for resawing, use a wide blade (½ inch wide or wider) with a coarse pitch (few teeth/inch). A blade with a pitch of 4–6 will work well. Fewer teeth leave more room for sawdust to be removed between the teeth, so a coarse blade can cut faster without clogging up.

Use a push stick at the end of the pass, to keep your fingers away from the blade (Illus. 5-11).

Illus. 5-9. Make sure that the fence is parallel to the blade by measuring the distance to the mitre slot at both ends of the fence as you clamp it.

Illus. 5-10. A little wedge of wood will keep the kerf open and prevent the blade from binding between the resawn boards.

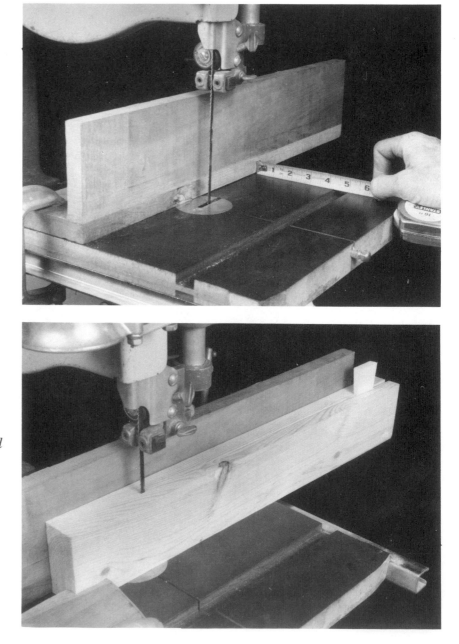

Illus. 5-11. A push stick is essential at the end of the pass to keep your fingers away from the blade.

Cutting Curves

When you're making toys, there are a lot of curves to cut. If you're planning to get into production work, you may want to consider where you need to be extremely accurate (cut slowly and carefully) and where you can move more quickly.

The areas around wheels and peg holes are critical for strength, and some lines, like the teeth on the shark project in Chapter 10, need to be clean and neat to give the toy an authentic look. The line of the shark's belly, however, could be off as much as ⅛ inch and it wouldn't matter.

This is not to suggest that you become less than diligent when woodworking. But if you're thinking of making toys for an income, you'll want to develop efficient cutting techniques in which you will make precise cuts only where they are necessary.

When cutting out parts with the band saw, always leave the pencil line, especially in critical areas, so that you can sand to the line when you're edge-sanding the silhouette.

There are some techniques that will yield better results when you are cutting curves. Keep in mind that the width of the blade is going to determine how tight a curve you can cut. This is easily learned by simply cutting. You'll feel the blade bind up or even burn if you try to turn too sharply.

If you're cutting an inside curve tighter than the blade will turn, there are several techniques you can use (Illus. 5-12–5-19). Illus. 5-20–5-22 show how to safely and effectively cut an outside curve that is too tight for the blade.

Any time that you make a curved cut that releases a little piece, turn the saw off and wait until it *stops* before you reach in to pull the scrap out (Illus. 5-23).

If you have to back out of a curved cut, turn the

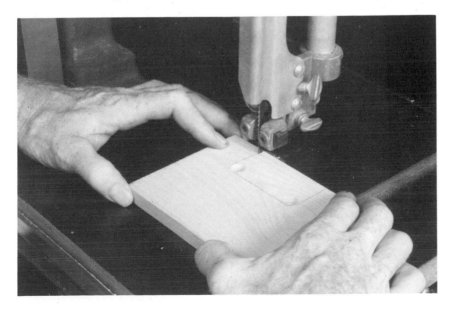

Illus. 5-12. You can drill holes at turning points of tight inside curves to enable you to cut them out in one pass. Try to match the hole diameter with the size of the curve for a clean corner.

Illus. 5-13. You can make straight relief cuts into a tight inside corner. (See Illus. 5-14.)

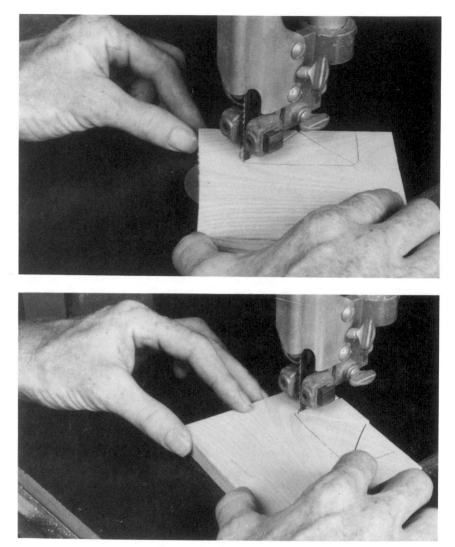

Illus. 5-14. Then the scrap will be released when you reach that line, enabling you to continue.

Illus. 5-15. Another method of cutting curves with a band saw. First, cut to the corner, as shown here. (See Illus. 5-16 and 5-17.)

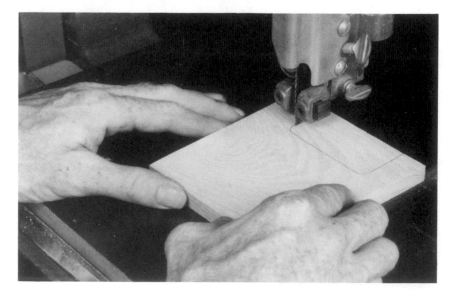

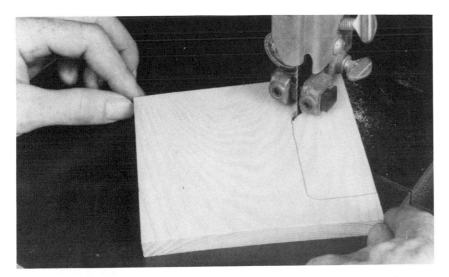

Illus. **5-16.** *Next, nibble away at the corner.*

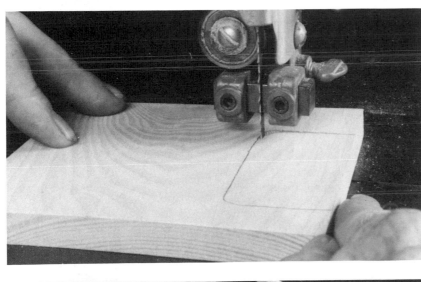

Illus. **5-17.** *Then change direction in the nibbled areas and cut across the bottom line to the other corner.*

Illus. **5-18.** *In this method of cutting inside curves, cut to the corner with the first cut and back out. Then sweep down towards the bottom and across the curve. (See Illus. 5-19.)*

Illus. **5-19.** *Then cut down into the other corner and back out. Start the next cut pretty low to the previous sweeping cut and meet the third cut. Make one more cut across the bottom, nibble slightly at the corner, and the curve will be complete.*

Illus. **5-20.** *Several straight relief cuts will enable you to cut tight outside curves by releasing the scrap when you complete the cuts.*

Illus. **5-21.** *Make several straight tangent cuts.*

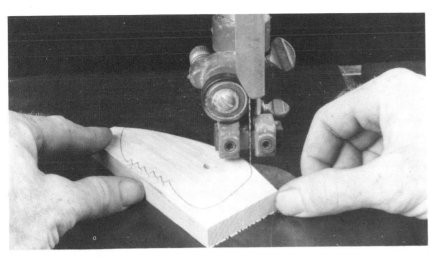

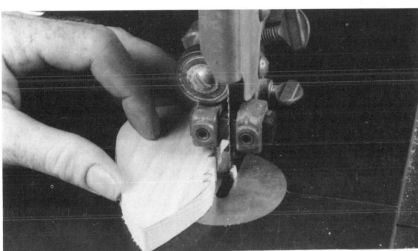

Illus. 5-22. Follow the curve until it gets too tight and then continue off the edge of the piece.

Illus. 5-23. If a piece of scrap is released and slips between the insert and the blade, turn the saw off and wait until it stops before you reach in for the piece.

saw off and wait until the saw stops. If you back out with the saw on, the sides of the cut may grab the set in the teeth and pull the blade towards you (*and off the wheels*).

When cutting on the band saw, it is extremely important that you keep your fingers out of the path of travel of the blade. Illus. 5-24 shows the wrong way to cut. If your hand were to slip (as you push), your thumb would go right into the blade. The correct way to cut is shown in Illus. 5-25. The piece should be held lightly by its edges or corners.

Crosscutting

Quite often, in toymaking, you will need to do repetitive cutoff work. Cutting dowels to length for axles and cutting wooden blocks to length are two good examples.

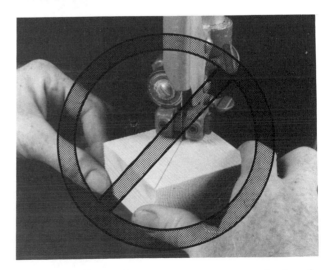

*Illus. 5-24. This is the **wrong** way to cut on the band saw. If your hand were to slip as it pushes forward, your thumb would go right into the blade.*

*Ilus. 5-25. This is the **correct** way to cut. Hold your work by its corners or edges to keep your fingers out of the path of travel of the blade. Use this cutting technique when using the scroll saw.*

You can make a very simple jig to do this operation safely. If you set the dowels right against the rip fence and push them by the blade with the crosscut guide, they will bind up as they pass the blade. They can get yanked downwards by the blade (Illus 5-26).

Set the fence by measuring from the blade to a scrap set next to the fence. Then slide the scrap towards you, well in front of the blade. Make sure that the clamp won't interfere with the wood being measured. Clamp the wood to the fence. This way, the length of the dowel or block will be positioned by the scrap against the fence, but the work will not be against the fence as it passes the blade (Illus. 5-27). You must still be careful, though, that a cut piece of dowel does not roll back into the blade and get caught.

When the cut is finished, slide the fence back, push the next block or set of axles against the scrap, and repeat the cuts. Note that in Illus. 5-28 there's a box to catch the cutoff pieces as they fall off the back of the table.

Band-Saw Safety Techniques

Follow these instructions when using a band saw:

1. Always wear safety glasses. Roll your sleeves up past your elbows and tuck in shirttails. Tie back long hair and don't wear loose jewelry.

2. Make sure the tension is set and the blade is tracking properly (Illus. 5-2 and 5-3).

3. Make sure that the guides are set properly (Illus. 5-4–5-6).

4. Keep your fingers out of the blade's path of travel (Illus. 5-24–5-26).

*Illus. 5-26. This is the **wrong** way to crosscut. Do not use the crosscut guide with your work against the rip fence or the workpiece will bind up between the blade and the fence and get yanked downwards or sideways.*

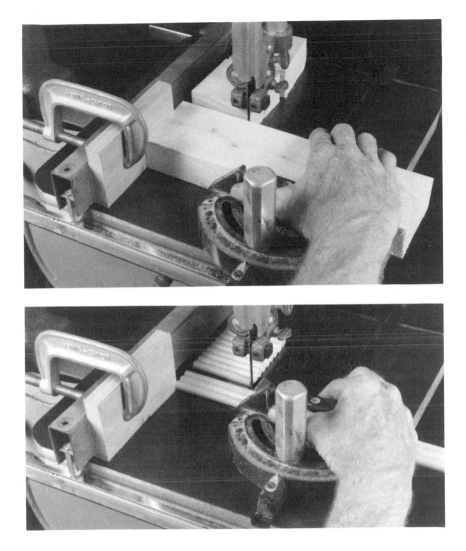

Illus. **5-27.** *Use a piece of scrap against the fence to measure the length of the fence. When the workpiece gets to the blade, the scrap is no longer there for the work to bind against.*

Illus. **5-28.** *You can repeat this process over and over without the work binding.*

5. Don't back out of tight curves with the saw running. Turn the saw off and wait until it stops.

6. Don't reach into the moving blade to remove scraps. Turn the saw off and wait until it stops (Illus. 5-23).

7. Don't use the crosscut guide with the wood against the rip fence (Illus. 5-26 and 5-27).

8. Use a push stick when resawing (Illus. 5-11).

9. Make sure the rip fence, or any jigs, are securely clamped in position before cutting.

Scroll Saw

The scroll saw is a handy tool for fine work like jigsaw puzzles, small toy parts, and cutout figures. A few simple adjustments have to be made to the scroll saw before it can be used. These consist of squaring the table to the blade and applying the proper tension to the blade.

To square the table to the blade, simply check it with a square or a square object and adjust it accordingly. Most saws have an adjustable mechanism for keeping the table square, such as a bolt on the bottom of the table. To adjust the table, adjust the bolt.

Adjusting the tension is not as cut and dry as squaring the table to the blade. The blade is too loose if it does not "twang" when plucked like a guitar string (Illus 5-29), it won't follow the line when you're cutting, or is noisy or vibrates a lot. The blade is too tight if it sounds extremely tight when plucked or when blades break frequently.

Illus. 5-29. The blade should "twang" when plucked, like a guitar string.

Also, make sure that your hold-down is set with enough tension to hold the wood down as the blade tries to lift it up and down while sawing.

Cutting Inside Areas

This is one of the operations that a scroll saw can do and a band saw cannot. A scroll-saw blade can be fed through a hole drilled in the work, and then set into the saw again (Illus. 5-30). Watch the tension as you reattach the blade.

Blades

If you use coping-saw blades, they will be too long for the scroll saw, so cut them to length (5 inches) with side cutters or lineman's pliers. This will also remove the pins in the ends that would otherwise get in the way (Illus. 5-31).

Whether you use coping-saw blades or scroll-saw blades, you'll need to decide what pitch (teeth per inch) is appropriate. Blades are available with pitches from 9.5 (size #12) to 28 (size #2/0). The finer the pitch (more teeth per inch), the more slowly the blade will cut, and the smoother will be the finished edge. Extremely fine blades can make a cut that doesn't require sanding. The coarser the pitch (fewer teeth per inch), the faster the blade will cut and the rougher the finished edge (Illus 5-32).

Use blades with a pitch of 11–11.5 (sizes #8, #9, and #10) for cutouts that will be edge-sanded. For finer work that is extremely hard to edge-sand, such as jigsaw puzzles, use a finer blade with a pitch of 13–14 (size #5 or #6). When you become used to working with these blades, experiment with others.

Safety Techniques

As with the band saw, the main danger in using a scroll saw is putting your fingers into the moving blade. The best way to prevent this from happen-

Illus. 5-30. By feeding the scroll-saw blade through your work and reattaching it, you can cut inside areas that the band saw won't reach.

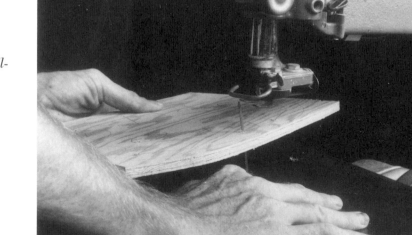

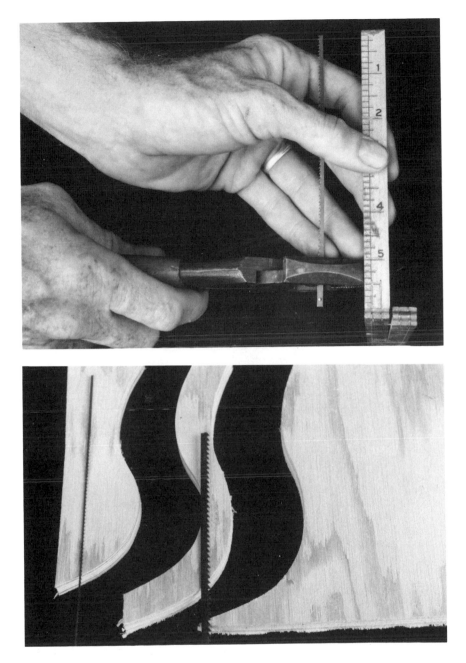

Illus. 5-31. *You will have to remove the pins on the end of coping-saw blades to use them on the scroll saw. Also, cut the blades so that they are five inches long.*

Illus. 5-32. *A coarse blade will cut faster and leave a rough edge, while a fine blade will cut more slowly and leave a smoother edge.*

ing is to keep your fingers out of the cutting path of the blade. With a little thought, you can feed any board through without pushing your fingers towards the blade.

Portable Jigsaw

The portable jigsaw is not really an essential tool for toymakers, but it can prove handy when making large curved cuts (Illus. 5-33). You can also use it to get started in toymaking if you don't have a band saw.

When using portable jigsaws, it is difficult to get a cut that is at right angles with the surface. Several things can be done to help solve this problem:

1. Use a coarse (few teeth per inch) blade that is stiff (Illus. 5-34).
2. Make sure that the blade is square to the worktable (Illus. 5-35).

Illus. 5-33. The portable jigsaw is great for pieces that are too large to cut on the band saw.

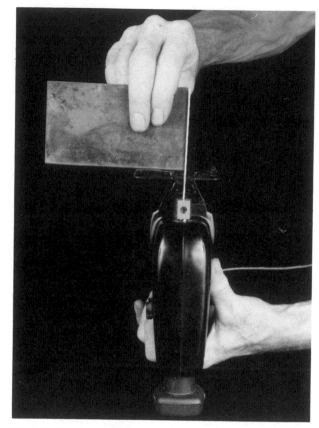

Illus. 5-35. Make sure that the blade is at right angles to the worktable.

3. Don't push the blade faster than it is capable of cutting.
4. Make sure that the worktable is flat to the work at all times. Do this by feeling the table.
5. Make sure that the scrap (or cutoff) is adequately supported as it is released, or it will bind the blade.

Coping Saw

To use the coping saw to cut out toy parts, you will have to mark, or position, the pattern on both sides of the wood. Drill axle holes or eye holes, etc., through the wood with the drill press and use those holes to position the pattern on the other side (Illus. 5-36). Next, put the work in a vise and keep the saw lined up with both patterns as you cut out the silhouette. Reposition it, and finish the cutout (Illus. 5-37 and 5-38).

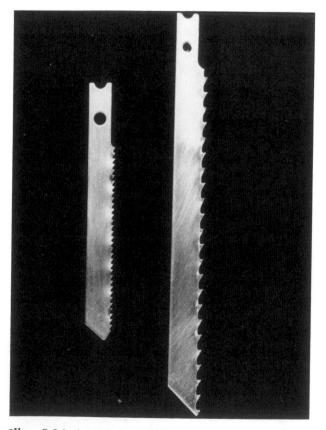

Illus. 5-34. A coarse, stiff blade will help to ensure a square cut. Note the dramatic difference in the size of the teeth on the blades.

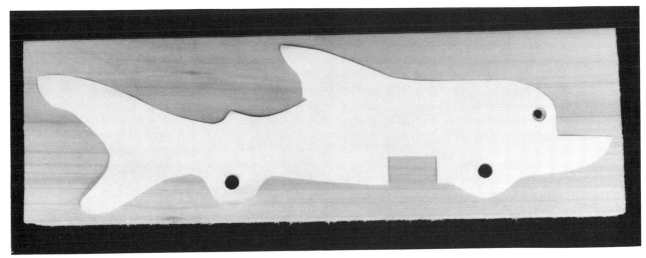

Illus. 5-36. *Punch holes in the pattern and use the holes in the workpiece to line the pattern up on the reverse side.*

Illus. 5-37. *Carefully follow the silhouette on both sides of your work.*

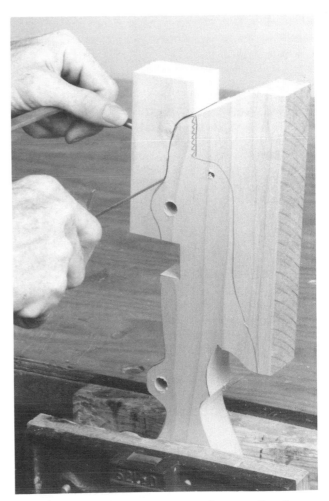

Illus. 5-38. *When the vise gets in the way, flip the piece over and finish the last cuts.*

Backsaw (Dovetail Saw) and Flexible Handsaw

There are several things you should be aware of when using a small handsaw, whether or not it is flexible. First, you need to know if the saw is made to cut on the push or the pull stroke (Illus 5-39). Japanese saws (and tools in general) are usually designed to cut on the pull stroke, while Western saws (American, British, German, etc.) are generally designed to cut on the push stroke.

Whichever way the saw is made to cut, it is easiest to get the cut started properly by gently pulling it across the line to create a slot for the saw to run in. Then continue with either push or pull strokes.

Quite often it is important that the end of the dowel, etc., be square. Watch the angle from both the vertical and the horizontal to make sure you are cutting a square end (Illus. 5-40).

When you have sawed almost completely through the cutoff, cut more quickly and push

Illus. 5-40. Dowels can be cut out-of-square if you're not careful when you're cutting them by hand. Watch both the vertical and horizontal planes.

Illus. 5-39. Looking at the angle of the teeth, you can see that the saw on the left is designed to cut on the pull stroke, while the saw on the right is made to cut on the push stroke.

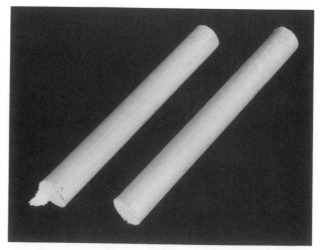

Illus. 5-41. The dowel on the left was sawn through with too much downward pressure at the end of the cut. The dowel on the right was sawn properly, with light, fast strokes at the end of the cut.

down very lightly. This will produce a smoother finish and avoid splintered ends (Illus. 5-41).

Finally, if you are cutting off a dowel flush to a piece of wood, keep in mind that the back of a backsaw will tend to set the blade at an angle to the surface of the wood unless it is off the edge of your work (Illus. 5-42 and 5-43). Again, here is the place where a flexible saw can cut flush without the back interfering (Illus 5-44).

Illus. 5-42. The "back" on a dovetail saw or backsaw will set the blade at an angle and will not cut the dowel off flush to the work surface.

Illus. 5-43. If the "back" is off the edge of the work, it will let the blade sit flush to the surface.

Illus. 5-44. A flexible saw enables you to easily cut dowels off flush to the work surface.

Chapter 6
DRILLING

Drilling holes can be a big part of toymaking. Some toys require accurate holes or holes at difficult angles, while others need large or multiple holes. All of these operations can be done smoothly if you know the drill bits that are best for toymaking, a few drilling techniques, and have some simple jigs.

Drill Bits for the Toymaker

The most common drill bit is the *twist bit* (Illus. 6-1). The flutes that spiral up the sides serve to clear the chips from the hole as it's drilled. This type of bit cuts quickly and makes a fairly clean hole. If you are drilling into extremely hard wood, or wood with a pronounced grain pattern, the bit may tend to wander as it starts the hole or even shift diagonally as it's drilling (Illus. 6-2). Large twist bits are also very expensive.

The *spade bit* (or speed bore) is made without much steel or machining, so it's quite inexpensive, especially for drilling large holes (Illus. 6-3). The spur in the center keeps it in line as the leading edges of the bit scrape out the hole. The hole is accurate, but the edges of the hole are rough. The four cutting surfaces of the spade bit

Illus. 6-1. The most common drill bit is the twist bit. It has a bevelled tip and flutes running its entire length to pull the chips up out of the hole as it drills.

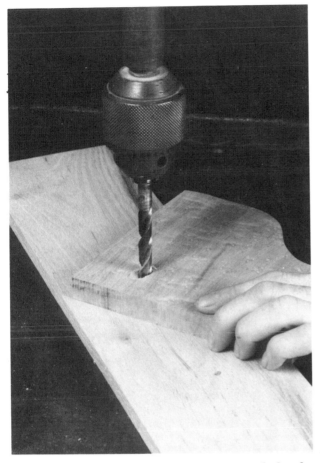

Illus. 6-2. When you're drilling into extremely hard wood, or even soft wood with a pronounced grain pattern (such as hard summer growth in pine), the bit may wander or shift as you are drilling.

Illus. 6-3. The spade bit is an inexpensive bit for drilling large holes.

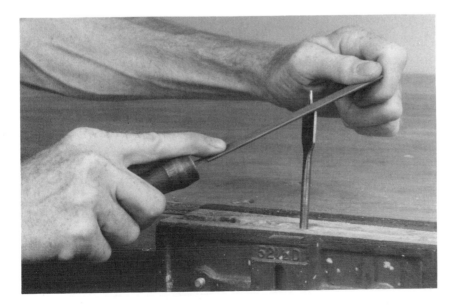

Illus. 6-4. You can use a flat file to sharpen the cutting edges of the spade bit.

Illus. 6-5. You can use a flat file to sharpen the sides of the leading point.

are flat and can be easily sharpened by hand with a flat file (Illus. 6-4 and 6-5).

Both the *brad-point bit* and the *Forstner bit* will produce an extremely accurate hole with clean sides (Illus. 6-6). Both types of bit have a little sharp point in the center (to keep the bit from wandering) and a leading spur (or two) on the outer edge to cut the outside edge of the hole cleanly. They will drill into wood at an angle smoothly and without wandering (Illus. 6-7).

The brad-point bit has a scraping type of cut similar to that produced by the tip of a twist drill. It cuts slightly more slowly than the Forstner bit, but its flutes help to remove most of the chips from the hole.

The Forstner bit has a knife-like cutter that does the actual drilling, so it cuts more aggressively than a brad-point bit. However, it has no flutes to carry the chips away, so you have to back out of the hole more frequently to keep the bit from bogging down with chips.

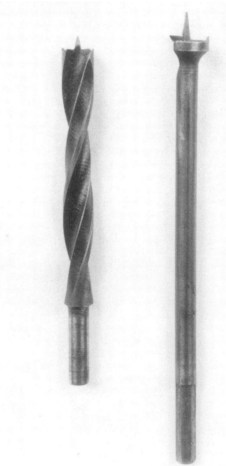

Illus. 6-6 (right). The brad-point bit (on the left) and the Forstner bit (on the right) both have a sharp point in the center and a spur (or spurs) on their outside edges. These features keep the bits from wandering and produce a hole with clean sides.

Either a *hole saw* or a *flycutter* will be essential if you are going to make your own wheels. The use of these bits is outlined on pages 59–61 (Illus. 6-21–6-34).

Basic Drilling Techniques

If you do any production toymaking, you may want to make a stand in which to store your most frequently used bits (Illus. 6-8).

Preventing Tear-Out

When you drill all the way through a piece of wood, the bit tends to splinter the wood in front of it as it breaks through the other side (Illus. 6-9). If you put scrap under your work, it supports the edges of the hole as the bit passes through, preventing "tear-out."

If the scrap shifts slightly between one hole and

Illus. 6-8. A stand for your most commonly used bits will speed up production.

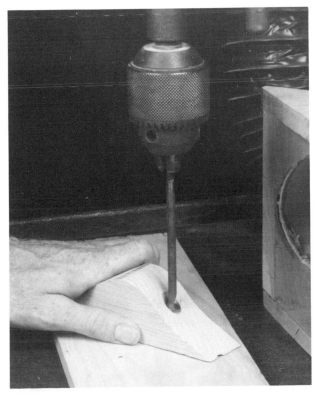

Illus. 6-7. Both the brad-point bit and the Forstner bit will drill into wood at an angle to the surface without being deflected.

Illus. 6-9. If you do not put scrap under your work, the bit will push splintered edges out the bottom of the hole as it comes through.

the next, it will no longer support the edges of the hole. Therefore, you should clamp the scrap if you're doing repetitive work (Illus. 6-10). This way, the wood will be supported each time the bit passes through the work.

Illus. 6-10. Clamping your scrap to the worktable is a good idea for repetitive drilling, to ensure that the edges of each new hole are supported by the scrap.

Clearing Chips

When you drill, the bit cuts a hole and the chips exit the hole. Both are essential to proper drilling.

The most common problem with drilling is the bit binding in the hole. This is usually caused by the chips not escaping quickly enough from the hole. If you drill partway in and pull the bit *all* the way out, you will give the bit a chance to clear all those chips. Then drill farther, clear the bit, and repeat the procedure. With a little experience, you'll know when to clear the bit and how quickly you can feed the bit into the work.

Depth of Hole

Whether you are drilling partway through your work or all the way through, the depth of the hole has to be set. (If you do not set the depth of cut, you can drill through the scrap into the worktable.)

Most drill presses have a set of threaded washers that can be used to determine how far down the drill bit will go (Illus. 6-11). When they are set, be sure to twist them in opposite directions to tighten them. If your drill press is not equipped with these washers, you can raise or lower the worktable until the bit drills as deep as you want it to. Another option is to buy stops for

Illus. 6-11. Use the threaded washers to set the depth of cut.

twist drills and brad-point bits that can be set for the proper depth of cut (Illus. 6-12). A further option is to make a stop by wrapping electrician's or masking tape around the bit at the proper depth. This method is very useful when you're using a portable electric drill (Illus. 6-13).

Drilling Jigs

Toymaking is an area of woodworking in which repetitive cuts are often made. Jigs will help to make repetitive work easier, more efficient, and more accurate. These jigs are almost essential if you're thinking about toymaking as a profession. Illus. 6-14–6-20 show very basic jigs that will prove helpful to toymakers.

Illus. 6-13. You can wrap tape around the drill bit to act as a depth stop.

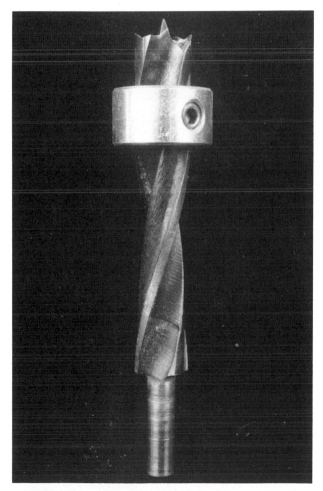

Illus. 6-12. Stops for drill bits are available which will help you control the depth of cut. These stops are especially helpful when you are drilling holes with a portable drill.

Illus. 6-14. Stops can be clamped onto the drill-press table for repetitive drilling.

Illus. 6-15.

Illus. 6-17. *The fence that you made for resawing on the band saw (see Chapter 5, Illus. 5-8 and 5-9) is quite handy for holding work accurately in a vertical position for drilling. You can add a stop for horizontal positioning.*

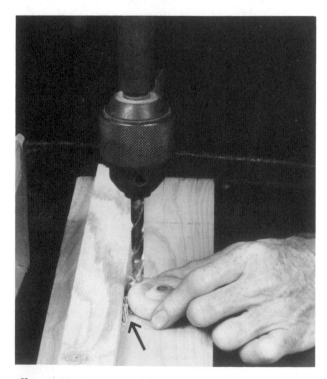

Illus. 6-16. *Be sure to blow away chips between each drilling or they will prevent the pieces from seating properly against the blocks.*

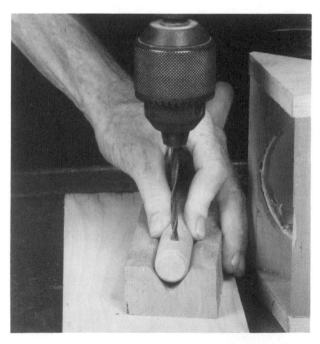

Ilus. 6-18. *A V-shaped slot in a piece of scrap will support a dowel and keep it from moving as you drill a hole through it. Use a brad-point or Forstner bit so that you can start the hole on a curved surface without the bit wandering.*

Illus. 6-19. If you use wheels with protruding hubs and you have to drill holes on the inside surface of the wheels, you can make a jig that will locate the wheel and let the wheel sit flat (with its hub sticking out). Drill a 1-inch hole about ¼ inch deep on a piece of wood with a spade bit. Place the wheel on the piece of wood so that its hub sits in the hole. Then place a board against the wheel to position it for drilling. Clamp the jig.

Illus. 6-20. To drill a hole in the end of a dowel to make a drum sander, drill a hole into the edge of a 2 × 4 that's slightly larger than the dowel you're drilling. Then clamp the board in the position shown here. You may have to hold the dowel with channel lock pliers to keep it from spinning as you drill. A folded piece of sandpaper (or a piece of inner tube) will protect the sides of the dowel from the jaws of the pliers. A center punch will help you to start the hole accurately.

Making Wheels Using a Hole Saw on the Drill Press

One arbor will fit any size hole saw (Illus. 6-21). Be sure to put a scrap under your work (to prevent tear-out around the axle hole). Drill about two-thirds of the way through (Illus. 6-22), flip the wood over, and drill the rest of the way through (Illus. 6-23). If you drill all the way through from one side, the bit will get caught in the wood and you'll have a difficult time removing the wheel.

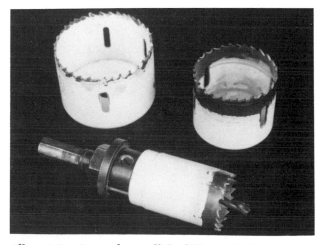

Illus. 6-21. One arbor will fit different hole saws to make different-size wheels.

Illus. 6-22. Drill about two-thirds of the way through.

Illus. 6-23. After drilling two-thirds of the way through, flip the board over and drill through from behind. This way, you have a large portion of the wheel to hold on to as you twist it off (clockwise).

Making Wheels Using a Flycutter on the Drill Press

A flycutter is infinitely variable and will make any size wheel. You may have to drill a pilot hole first (if the pilot is not a drill bit). Make sure that the wheel is properly located so that the cutter won't go off the edge of the board. The cutter can face in two directions. Place its long edge next to the wheel's tread so there is no bevelled scrap left on the wheel's tread (Illus. 6-24).

Illus. 6-24. Note that the cutter is set with its long edge inward, so that the bevelled scrap is not left on the edge of the wheel.

The flycutter is dangerous because of the heavy arm that the cutter is set into. If it were to hit your hand, you could be seriously injured. Make sure that you clamp your board to the drill press and keep your hands clear of the flycutter (Illus. 6-25).

The flycutter is slow because one cutter is doing all the work and is actually scraping rather than cutting. Therefore, run the drill press at a slow speed, keep the cutter sharp, and don't try to lower the cutter too quickly.

To make the wheel with a flycutter, drill halfway through, and then flip the board over to finish the

Illus. 6-25. *Note that the board is clamped to the drill-press table so that the operator's hands will be clear of the spinning cutter.*

wheel. Make sure that the scrap under your work has a hole that the pilot can go into (if the pilot is not a drill bit), because it sticks down farther than the cutter and will come through the board first.

Making Wheels with the Band Saw or Scroll Saw

First, mark the center of the wheel for drilling. Then, with a compass, scribe the size wheel that you want. If you need very large wheels, you may want to glue and screw pieces of plywood together to make thicker, stronger wheels. Make sure that there are no screws near the center, where the axle will be drilled. Countersink the screws deeply enough to cover them with a plug or dowel if you're planning a clear finish or water putty if you're going to paint the wheels.

For wheels that are larger than a compass can scribe, you can use one of two techniques. In the first method, mark the center and tack a looped end of string to that point. Make a loop at the other end of the string and place a pencil through that loop to mark the outside of the circle (Illus. 6-26).

In the second method, find an object that is the

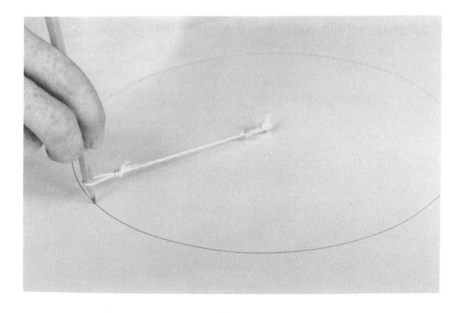

Illus. 6-26. *You can make a large compass using a piece of string with a loop at both ends, a tack, and a pencil. Make sure that the string spins freely and the pencil stays vertical, or you may not be able to draw an accurate circle.*

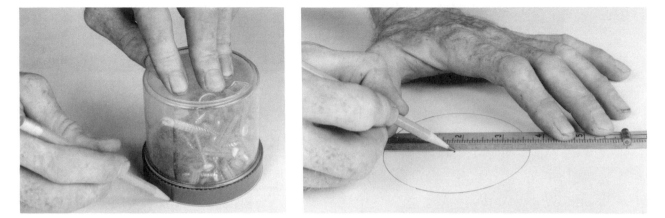

Illus. 6-27 (above left). An object in the workshop or house might provide the size circle you're looking for. Illus. 6-28 (above right). To locate the center of the wheel, draw a line at the thickest part of the circle, and mark the middle of the line.

right size and trace around it (Illus. 6-27). Then draw a line across the center (the thickest part of the circle), measure halfway across, and draw a second line at right angles to the first (Illus. 6-28). This will be the center of the wheel.

Next, drill the axle hole all the way through the center, with a scrap of wood under your work to prevent tear-out. Then cut the wheel out on the band saw or scroll saw, leaving the pencil line as a guide for sanding.

Finishing the Wheels

No matter which method you use to make your wheels, you'll want to edge-sand the tread surface. If you used the hole saw or the flycutter, edge-sanding lightly will remove any burrs or roughness. If you used the band saw or scroll saw, you can use the pencil line to help you smooth out any irregularities in the circular shape (Illus. 6-29).

The last step is to round the edge over where the tread and the sidewall meet. On small wheels, this is done by simply sanding the edges at a 45-degree angle with #120-grit paper to break the edge (Illus. 6-30).

On the larger wheels, the edges can be rounded using a rasp (Illus. 6-31), a file (Illus. 6-32), and sandpaper (Illus. 6-33), or the router with a quarter-round bit and a router mat (Illus. 6-34). (See pages 83–86 for information on routing.)

You'll probably need to hand-sand the routed edges.

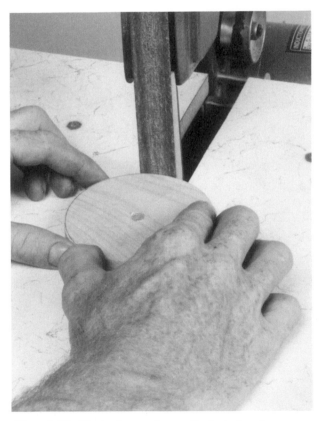

Illus. 6-29. If you leave the scribed circle when you cut out your wheels, you can use that line as a guide when you're sanding to smooth out any irregularities.

Illus. 6-30. The sharp edge is broken by hand-sanding with #120-grit paper at a 45-degree angle.

Illus. 6-31. The rasp will quickly round over the edges of large wheels.

Illus. 6-32. The file will smooth rough rasp marks.

Illus. 6-33. Hand-sand the rounded edges for a smooth finish.

Illus. 6-34. The edges of large wheels can be rounded over with the router and a router mat, for those with experience with the router.

Chapter 7
SANDING

If any one of the toymaking techniques could be singled out as the most important, it would be sanding. Unlike many other woodworking projects, toys are almost always made to be handled, so how a toy feels is very important. It must be "splinter-free" to be *safe* to play with, but it must also be smooth to the touch to be *fun* to play with.

Although how the toy works is the real basis for its success, the appearance of a toy is also vital to attracting and holding a child's interest. The well-sanded toy has more visual appeal than a rough cutout. Basically, a properly sanded toy is more fun to play with and is much more likely to be used.

Toys come in so many different shapes and sizes that many different sanding techniques must be used. Because so much sanding is involved, you will soon get frustrated trying to do much of your serious sanding by hand. It will be much more helpful if you use a 1-inch sander/grinder (or edge sander) to sand the edges of toy parts or silhouettes and a 4–6-inch-wide belt sander (stationary or hand-held) to sand flat surfaces. If you are planning to make toys for income, you'll find that belt sanders are essential. The added time spent hand-sanding will either make your toys too expensive or your income negligible.

There are also several attachments for the drill press that will speed up your sanding, as well as ensure consistent sanding quality (Illus. 7-1).

Illus. 7-1. *There are several sanding devices available that are used on the drill press.*

The 1-inch Sander/Grinder

The 1-inch sander/grinder (or edge sander) is used to sand the edges of toy parts (or the silhouette). The edges are usually sanded before the flat surfaces so that you can use your pencil line or the edge of your glued-on pattern to sand to (Illus. 7-2). A drum sander on the drill press can also be used for these surfaces. A drum sander has an advantage in that it can sand with the grain. However, it clogs up with sawdust very quickly and does not sand nearly as fast as the sander/grinder.

Adjusting the Sander/Grinder

The tension on the 1-inch sander is set automatically by a spring in the arm that supports the upper wheel. The belt should ride (or "track") in the center of the wheels or pulleys. How this is done will depend on the particular sander.

The 1-inch sander has a small worktable that can be adjusted to different angles. Most of the time, this worktable has to be at right angles to the belt, so that the edges can be sanded perpendicular to the surfaces. Simply hold a square to the table and adjust the table accordingly (Illus. 7-3).

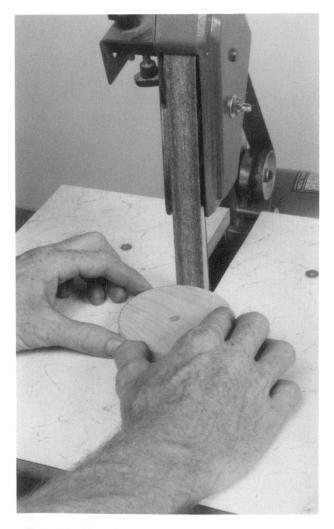

Illus. 7-2. The edges are sanded before the flat surfaces. This way, you can use the pencil lines as a guide for accuracy.

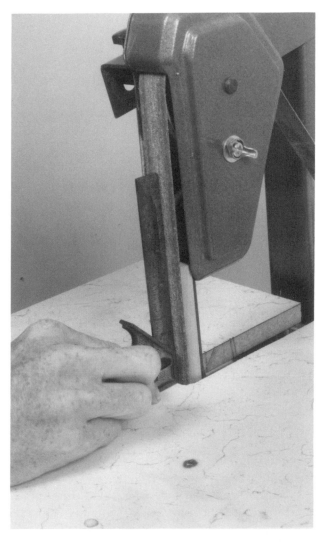

Illus. 7-3. Make sure that the worktable is perpendicular to the sanding belt or the edges won't be square.

Platens

The belt is supported from behind with a platen. Most 1-inch sanders are equipped with a flat platen. A flat platen will work excellently on outside curves, but not so well for inside curves (Illus. 7-4).

I modified my platen so that it will sand inside curves of 1-inch radius or more. I split a 1-inch-thick dowel and used it to change my flat platen into a curved platen (Illus. 7-5–7-8). Unfortunately, the heat generated during sanding will burn the dowel and it will have to be replaced from time to time. A half cylinder of steel screwed or brazed to the platen would last indefinitely.

Sanding with the Sander/Grinder

The sander/grinder is used to edge-sand. Edge-sanding is done to remove any saw marks, to smooth out rough, uneven lines, or to make the edges smooth to the touch.

Edge-sanding is generally done in at least two passes. The first pass is usually made with a #80-grit belt. This pass will remove saw marks and clean up the line (Illus. 7-9). There are some areas where accuracy in sanding is critical. As examples, a certain amount of wood is required around axles and peg holes to ensure strength; some pieces have to be specific shapes for clearances with other pieces and for proper movement; and

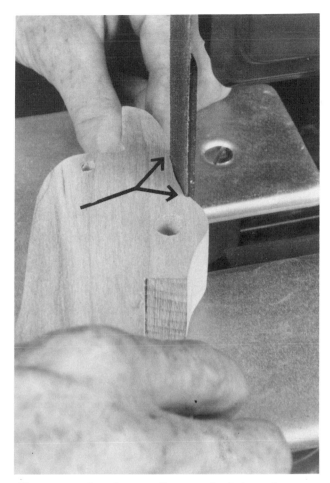

Illus. 7-4. A flat platen will cause the belt to dig into the edges of inside curves.

Illus. 7-5. A scrap of wood with a V-shaped notch cut into it will help you rip a 1-inch-thick dowel in half to make a curved platen.

Illus. 7-6. *Two holes are drilled through the platen and the dowel so that they can be screwed together from the back.*

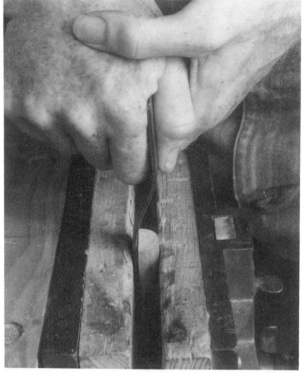

Illus. 7-7. *Then the platen is bent in a vise so that the front of the curved platen will be where the flat platen was (behind the belt).*

Illus. 7-8. *Screw the dowel half to the platen.*

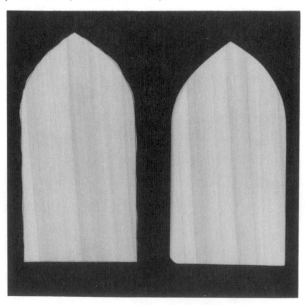

Illus. 7-9. *At left is a board before the first pass is made. At right is a board after the first pass is made. Note the difference. The first pass removes any saw marks and smooths any irregularities in the line.*

the pieces on some toys have to be shaped precisely to make the toy appear convincing (Illus. 7-10–7-12).

In some places, however, your sanding can be as much as ⅛ inch off the line and it really won't matter, as long as the line is smooth (Illus 7-13).

There is no point in spending a lot of time being unduly careful if it's not necessary. If you are thinking of making toys to sell them, this is an important point in terms of keeping their price down.

It is important that you remove any saw marks

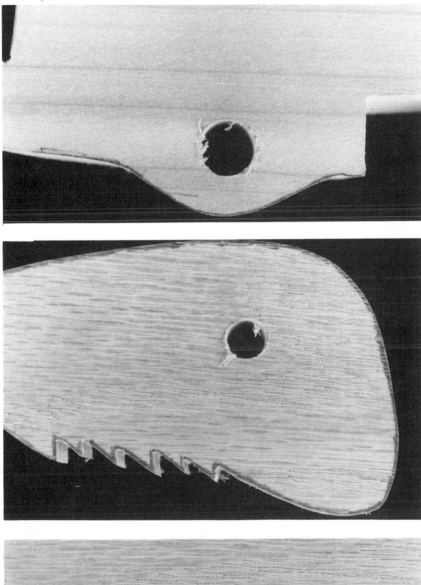

Illus. 7-10. The sanding around the axle holes and peg holes on this shark toy (described in Chapter 10) needs to be accurate to ensure strength.

Illus. 7-11. Areas that relate to movement (like this base for the shark toy's jaw) need to be shaped accurately so that the parts will move smoothly.

Illus. 7-12. In some places, the accuracy of the line is what gives the toy its convincing appearance. Detail can be important. Shown here are the teeth on the shark.

Illus. 7-13. In some places, as on the shark's belly, the line does not need to be accurate, and a smooth curve is all that's necessary.

and roughness with the #80-grit belt, because these marks will be much more difficult to remove with a #120-grit belt. Make the second pass (and/or third, etc.) with a #120-grit belt. This pass simply removes the scratches made by the previous belt. As you are sanding across the grain, use progressively finer belts until the cross-grain scratches virtually disappear.

When you sand with the sander/grinder, move the piece across the belt in a fluid motion. Any time you stop moving your work, the belt will flatten the line (Illus. 7-14). If the wood starts to burn, you are either pushing too hard against the belt or the belt is worn out. A light pass, or a new belt, will remove any burns.

For tight inside curves (no less than 1 inch in diameter), push the piece a little harder and very quickly to get the belt to conform to the shape of the curved platen and to prevent the piece from digging in at the edges of the belt.

In some areas, it's helpful to take the platen off altogether and use the edges of the belt to get into tight corners (Illus. 7-15). If you are planning to make toys to sell, time becomes a more serious factor and you may want to have two edge sanders, one with a platen and one without.

The belts on many sander/grinders can be fed through the work, so that the sander can be used to sand inside enclosed spaces (Illus. 7-16).

The sander/grinder is also handy for sharpen-

Illus. 7-14. Keep the work moving at all times or the areas will develop a flat spot.

Illus. 7-15. With the platen off, you can use the edges of the belt to get into tight corners.

Illus. 7-16. You can sand any inside cuts made by the scroll saw or jigsaw by feeding the belt through the work and remounting it on the top roller.

ing chisels, etc. Do not grind metal on the sander/grinder if a dust system is hooked up to it. If you do, the sparks can fly into the dust container and start a fire!

I found it helpful to build a larger worktable and screw it to the existing one. This gives additional support to larger pieces, making it easier to keep the work perpendicular to the belt and ensuring accurate work. It is best to screw the new table on from underneath, to avoid having any screw heads on the work surface.

6 × 48-inch Belt Sander

A 6 × 48-inch stationary belt sander is the ideal tool for production-sanding of flat surfaces. You can, however, use a portable belt sander, clamped securely upside down in a vise (Illus. 7-17).

Belt Direction

Before you can use your belt sander, you must make sure that the belt is running in the right direction. Most sanding belts have arrows on the back that show the proper direction of rotation. If they aren't marked, look at the joint where the ends of the belt are glued together. A butt joint can move in either direction without catching on the wood (Illus. 7-18). A lap joint, however, will

Illus. 7-17. The portable belt sander clamped (securely) in a vise, upside down, makes an adequate substitute for a stationary belt sander.

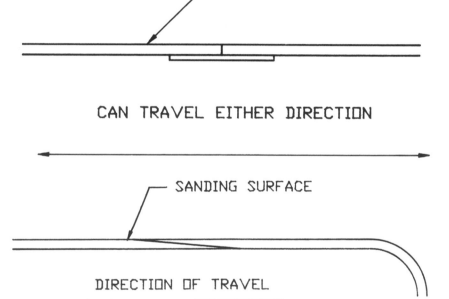

Illus. 7-18. A butt joint has no overlap to catch on your work, so the belt sander can be moved in either direction (across or up and down).

Illus. 7-19. Note that the overlap runs away from the work instead of into it. This way, the work won't get caught on the overlap and tear it apart.

catch on wood and tear the belt apart if you run the belt in the wrong direction. The lap joint should slope up and away from the direction of travel so that the joint tends to deflect off the edge of the wood instead of catching on it (Illus. 7-19).

Tension

After determining that the belts are running in the proper direction, the next step is to adjust their tension. Actual tension adjustments differ from sander to sander, so I won't go into detail. Basically, though, the belt should be tight, with a little flex in it. There should be enough slack so that you can squeeze the belt slightly and, when you release it, it returns to its original position. You will be able to apply the proper amount of tension through practice.

As Illus. 7-20 and 7-21 show, tension is checked at the non-drive end of the belt sander. You can make final adjustments in the tension as you set up the tracking.

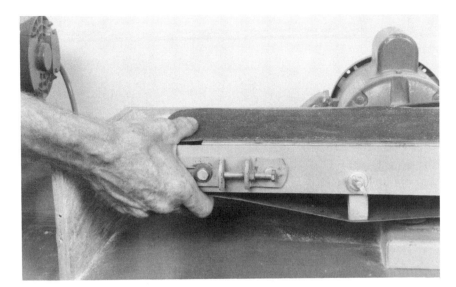

Illus. 7-20 and 7-21. The belt will have a proper amount of tension when you squeeze it, as shown here, and it returns to its original position when you let go, as shown in Illus. 7-21.

Illus. 7-21.

Tracking

The belt on the stationary sander should "track" on the center of the drums. Again, this adjustment differs from one sander to the next. Some sanders have adjustments on both sides of the drum and may have a V-shaped strip of metal underneath them that helps to keep the belt tracking properly (Illus 7-22 and 7-23). Other sanders (including most hand-held belt sanders)

Illus. 7-22 (right). Some sanders will have a tension adjustment on either side of the drum. This also adjusts the tracking.

Illus. 7-23. The V-shaped strip of metal under the sander also helps the belt track properly.

Illus. 7-24. The more common tracking adjustment is a knurled knob that tilts the non-drive wheel from side to side.

on either side of the drum if they go far enough off-center (Illus. 7-25). This will also fray the edges of the belts.

Illus. 7-25. If the belt tracks far enough off-center, it can cut into the metal on both sides and fray its edges.

have a pivot mechanism that tips the non-drive roller from side to side (Illus. 7-24).

Whether the drums or rollers are the same width as the belt or wider, the belt should ride in the center of the drums. If the belt is off to one side, it will move drastically off-center as soon as a piece of wood is pressed against it. As sandpaper belts are abrasive, they will cut through the metal

If the belt on a hand-held belt sander is not tracking properly, it can also extend out to the side of the sander. If this happens, the belt will no longer be supported entirely by the platen behind it, and only part of the belt will actually be sanding (Illus. 7-26). The belt can also fly right off the side of the sander.

Safety Guidelines

There are three safety concerns specific to the stationary belt sander. First, be careful how you hold your work as you press it onto the sander. If you extend your fingertip slightly beyond the bottom of your work, you may inadvertently sand it (Illus. 7-27).

Second, grip your wood firmly and don't press down too hard. Let the belt do the cutting. If you press hard and your hand slips, you will push your fingertips against the belt. Third, if a toy part is so small or thin that belt-sanding it makes you nervous, sand it by hand.

Sanding with the Stationary Belt Sander

If you look at a belt sander without the belt on, you'll see a drum (or pulley) at both ends and a platen (metal support) in the middle (Illus 7-28).

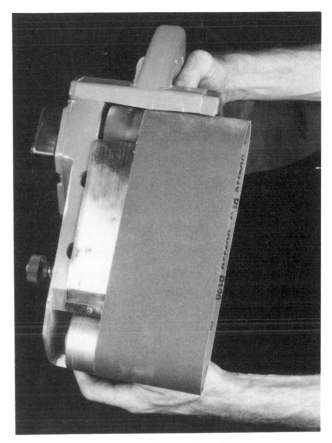

Illus. 7-26. An improperly tracking belt on a portable belt sander will not be supported by the platen and can also fly right off the sander.

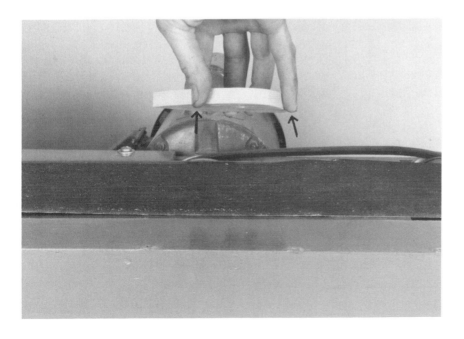

Illus. 7-27. Make sure that your fingertips don't extend beyond the bottom surface of your work as you press it down onto the sander. The sander will remove flesh extremely quickly!

Illus. 7-28. Note the platen in the middle and the drums at either end. Sanding is meant to be done over the platen only.

Illus. 7-29. If your work is held down over the roller, it will gouge the surface.

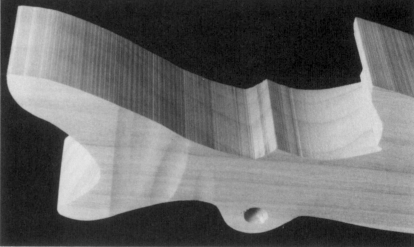

When sanding a surface flat, keep your work directly over the platen, where the belt is supported. If you press your work down over the roller, it will dig into your piece (Illus. 7-29).

When sanding a surface flat, make sure that the grain direction of your work is parallel to the belt's direction of travel. Toy parts are laid out with the grain, when possible, for strength. Sometimes, though, pieces may fit better on your board if they are slightly out of line with the grain (Illus. 7-30). Make sure that the grain runs parallel with the direction of the belt's travel, even if it is not exactly in line with the edges of the piece (Illus. 7-31).

Always move your piece from side to side as you sand (Illus. 7-32). This way, you use the entire width of the belt instead of just wearing out the center. Also, moving the piece back and forth along the belt gives the dust that you remove a chance to leave the belt instead of clogging the pores as you keep pressing it in. This will add greatly to the life of your belts.

When belt-sanding, you will generally graduate from a coarse belt (#80 grit) to a finer one (#120 grit), and further in some cases. The first sanding should remove any planer marks or marks made from resawing. Make sure that you remove all of these marks before you switch to a finer belt. If the #80-grit belt doesn't remove them, the #120-grit belt won't be able to. Use the #120-grit belt just to remove the scratches left by the #80-grit belt, not to remove planer marks, etc.

Illus. 7-30. The grain does not always run straight down your board, and quite often it will not run exactly straight along the toy part.

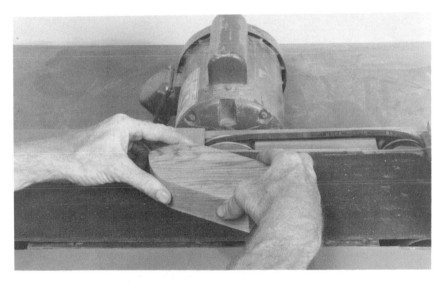

Illus. 7-31. Make sure that the grain *runs parallel with the direction of the belt's travel,* even if the piece is not straight.

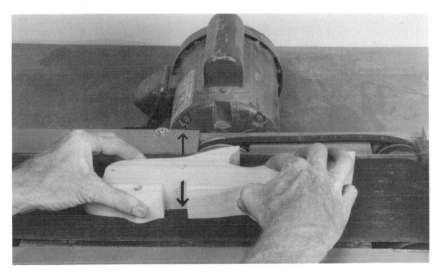

Illus. 7-32. Move your work from side to side as you sand it, to use the whole belt and to let the sawdust clear the belt.

Follow the same procedures if you are using a finer belt. A #180-grit belt will easily remove the scratches left by the #120-grit belt, but not those left by the #80-grit belt.

The results of the #80-grit belt are the easiest to see. After you have sanded a bit, flip the piece over and see where you have missed (Illus. 7-33). Remember that when you flip the piece back over you are reversing the position of the area that needs sanding (Illus. 7-34). As you continue sand-ing, *do not tip* the piece to the side that was missed or you'll end up with two flat surfaces instead of one (Illus. 7-35). Set the piece down flat on the sander and simply apply a little more pressure on the area that you missed. With a little practice, you'll get to the point where you only have to look at the surface once while sanding it flat, sand any missed areas, and then start sanding the other side.

Illus. 7-33. Note that the area missed by the sander is in the back when you look directly at the piece, as shown here, but is in the front when you flip the piece back over to continue sand-ing, as shown in Illus. 7-34. So put a little more pressure over this area to finish sanding it.

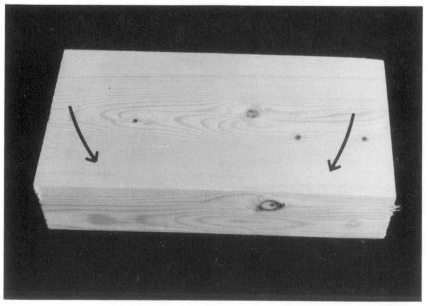

Illus. 7-34.

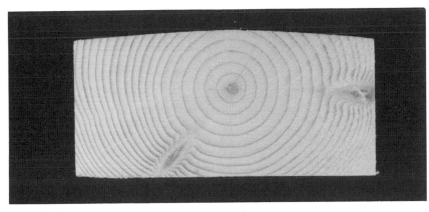

Illus. 7-35. Do not tip the piece in the direction of the missed area or you'll end up with two flat surfaces instead of one.

Portable Belt Sander

If you are sanding large pieces such as the parts to the Horse Glider described in Chapter 10, you will have to use a portable belt sander. Keep the belt sander moving with the grain, forward and back. Overlap your passes. Don't press down on the sander. Let the belt and the weight of the sander do the work.

You can clamp a block to the edge of your workbench to act as a stop. The stop should be thinner than your work so you can sand to the edges of your piece without interference. As Illus. 7-36 shows, the clamp should be off to the side so that the sander won't hit it.

By clamping work in the vise, you can also use the portable belt sander to edge-sand pieces that are too large for the 1-inch sander/grinder (Illus. 7-37).

Check between the pad and the platen of the portable belt sander for any accumulated sawdust and remove it. If you don't, it can build up into little bumps that will turn into indented grooves in your work.

Drill Press Attachments

Two sanding devices that can be attached to the drill press are the drum sander and the flap sander. The drum sander is a handy tool for edge-sanding. The rigid drum sander is made of a hard rubber cylinder with a bolt through it. As the bolt is tightened, the drum expands slightly, holding the sleeve securely in place. This type of drum sander is inexpensive and comes in many sizes

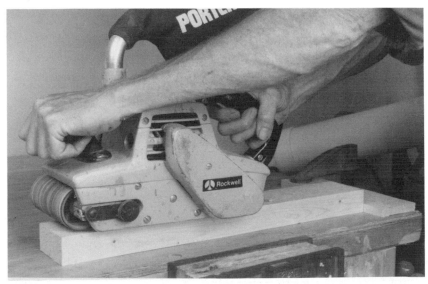

Illus. 7-36. A piece of scrap will make a great stop for belt-sanding. Note that it is thinner than the piece being sanded so that the belt sander can go right over it. Also, the clamp is off to the side so that it won't be in the way.

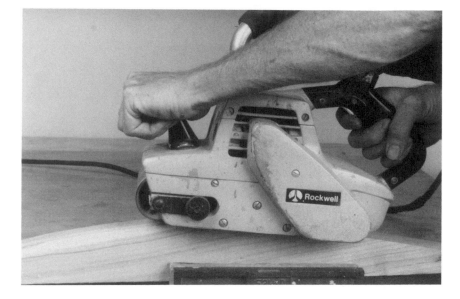

Illus. 7-37. Big outside curves can be sanded with the portable belt sander.

for different thicknesses of wood and different-diameter curves (Illus. 7-38). The sleeves come in different grits, so you can follow the same sequence of coarse-to-fine sanding as you would with the edge sander and the wide belt sander. The main disadvantage to these drum sanders is that they have so little surface area (compared to belt sanders) that they quickly clog up with sawdust. This makes it necessary to clean them quite often, so that they will be effective. (See Cleaning Sanding Belts, page 81.) They will, however, sand *with* the grain on the edges, unlike the edge sander, so they won't create cross-grain scratches.

You can also make a rigid drum sander with a piece of dowel. Cut a slot through the dowel and slip a piece of sandpaper in it. You can even make a drum sander bigger than the chuck opening on your drill press by drilling a hole in the slotted dowel and gluing a ⅜- or ½-inch dowel into it (Illus. 7-39).

Another attachment for the drill press is the flap sander. There are many different types of flap sander on the market. They are designed to flex and follow contours (Illus. 7-40).

Illus. 7-38. Rigid drum sanders are inexpensive and are available in many different sizes.

Illus. 7-39. You can make a drum sander by cutting a slot in a dowel and inserting sandpaper into it. Note the ⅜-inch-thick dowel in the end of the large slotted dowel. This way, you can make a drum sander of a larger diameter than the chuck opening of your drill press.

Illus. 7-40. Flap sanders will follow contours quite well.

Cleaning Belts and Drums

The belt cleaner is a relatively new tool. It is basically synthetic rubber that grabs the sawdust and pulls it off the sanding belt. If you clean your belts *frequently* (every one to two minutes of sanding), they will last up to ten times longer on hardwood. Unfortunately, belt cleaners will not remove all the resin associated with softwood, but they will remove the dust and some of the resin (Illus. 7-41).

Simply press the belt cleaner against the belt or drum while it is running until it returns to its original color.

Illus. 7-41. Use belt cleaners frequently to prolong belt life.

Rounding and Routing

The final step in the sanding process before hand-sanding is to round off the edges of toy parts. This will make them more pleasant to handle and less likely to cause splinters.

The edges on small parts can be rounded over by hand with sandpaper. (See Hand Sanding on pages 86–88). The edges of slightly larger pieces should be thoroughly rounded over. This can be done with sandpaper, with a rasp and file, or with a router.

Four-in-Hand

The four-in-hand (or shoe rasp) is a flat and curved rasp (for quick cutting) and a flat and curved file (to smooth rasp marks) (Illus. 7-42). Four-in-hands are available in 8- or 10-inch lengths. I find that 8-inch-long four-in-hands are suited to the size of the hand. The ends of the tool are rounded to make it comfortable to hold.

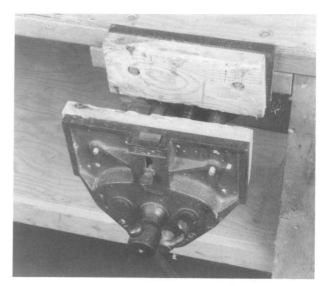

Illus. 7-43. Note the softwood that lines the jaw faces to minimize dents in the work.

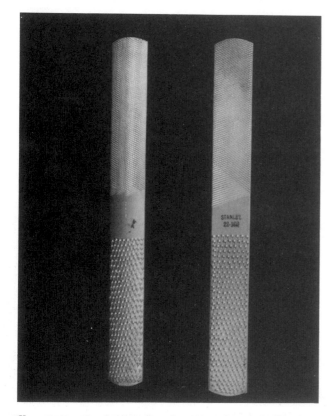

Illus. 7-42. The four-in-hand is a combination flat-and-curved rasp and flat-and-curved file.

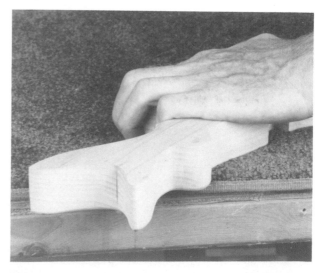

Illus. 7-44. A piece of carpet under your work will protect the sanded surfaces while you work with the four-in-hand.

Your work should be held firmly while you rasp and file. If you use a vise, it should have softwood attached to its jaw faces to prevent the metal from marring the surfaces (Illus. 7-43).

Some pieces can be held down firmly on the edge of the workbench. A piece of carpet under the work will prevent the bench from scratching the surfaces of the work (Illus. 7-44).

Files and rasps are made to cut on the push stroke. Do not drag the four-in-hand back over your work or you will flatten the teeth and shorten the life of the cutting edges. Lift the four-in-hand up at the end of a pass, bring it back to the beginning, and stroke again.

Unlike most sanding, this rasping and filing is best accomplished by working across the grain (Illus. 7-45).

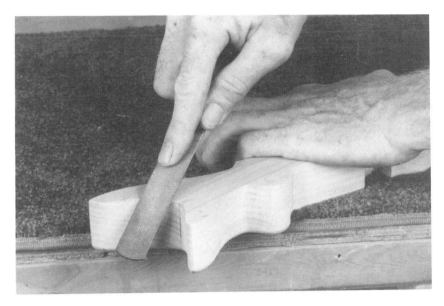

Illus. 7-45. Cut across the corners at about 45 degrees rather than with the grain.

Use the curved rasp for inside curves and the flat rasp for outside curves and flat areas. Then follow up with the corresponding file to smooth off the marks left by the rasp (Illus. 7-46). Be sure to remove all the rasp marks with the file, because the sandpaper will have a hard time removing them.

The teeth on the four-in-hand will get clogged with sawdust. You can remove sawdust with a small brush with stiff metal bristles. A hardware or plumbing supply store will sell a brush for cleaning the inside of copper pipe before soldering. A shoe repair store will sell a small brass brush for roughing up suede. Some woodworking catalogues carry file cards. Any of these will work fine (Illus. 7-47).

Using a Router

The router can be used to quickly round edges. Do not use this tool, however, unless you have experience with it. Following are guidelines for using the router to round edges.

You will only need one bit for this type of routing: a ¼-inch-radius, quarter-round bit. Plain steel bits do not stay sharp very long, and the tip of the bit that rides against the edge of the work will burn the surface (Illus. 7-48). Instead, use a carbide-tipped bit with a roller bearing (Illus.

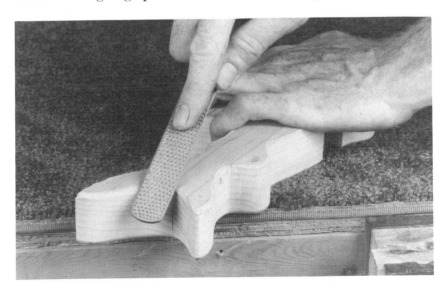

Illus. 7-46. The file will remove the rough marks left by the rasp.

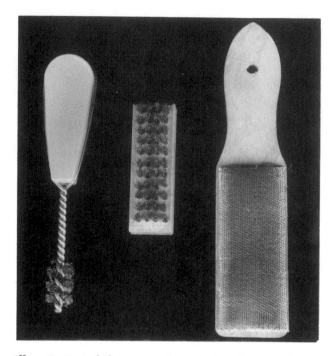

Illus. 7-47. At left is a metal brush for cleaning the inside of copper pipe prior to soldering. It can be found at a plumbing supply store. In the middle is a brass brush for roughing up suede. It can be found at a shoe repair store. On the right is a file card, which can be found in some woodworking catalogues. Any of these will clean the sawdust out of the teeth of the four-in-hand.

7-49). These bits are slightly more expensive, but they stay sharp longer and will not burn your work.

Because the bit spins quickly, it has a tendency to grab the work and fling it, so make sure the piece is securely held. Large pieces such as sheets of plywood will not be affected because they are heavy. Smaller pieces can be held in the vise, if they are thick enough that the bit won't hit the vise as it passes around the piece (Illus. 7-50).

Another option for small pieces is the router mat (available through most woodworking catalogues). This is a piece of high-density foam that your work sits on as you rout it. The foam grips the bottom of your work and keeps it from being flung away by the spinning bit (Illus. 7-51).

Remember that the bit is turning clockwise as you look down at your work. This means that you should move your router around your piece in a counterclockwise direction. This way, the rotation of the bit will be opposite the direction of travel of the router. If you move your router around the

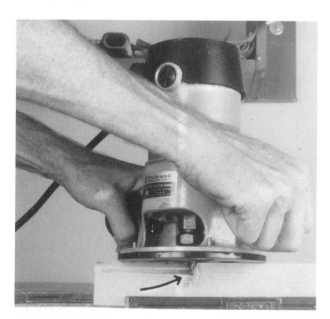

Illus. 7-48. The bearing surface of a steel router bit will burn your work.

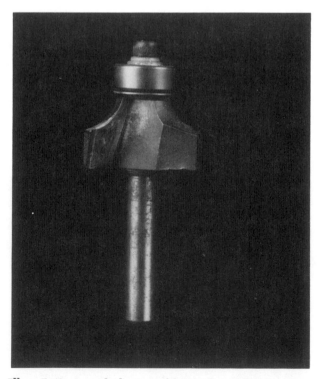

Illus. 7-49. A carbide-tipped bit with a roller bearing will stay sharp longer, and the roller bearing reduces burns on the silhouette of the work.

piece in a clockwise direction, the bit will rotate and the router will travel in the same direction, and the router bit will be propelled along the edge of the wood, forcing you to lose control (Illus 7-52 and 7-53).

LOOKING DOWN AT A ROUTER ON TOP OF YOUR WORK .....

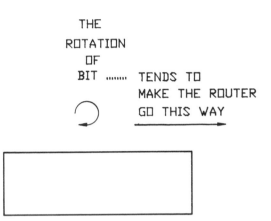

THE
ROTATION
OF
BIT .... TENDS TO
MAKE THE ROUTER
GO THIS WAY

Illus. 7-52. If you move the router clockwise around your work, the router will be propelled along the edge of your work.

SO .....

FEED THE
ROUTER
THIS WAY
(COUNTER CLOCKWISE) .....

TO COUNTERACT
ITS TENDANCY
TO GO THIS WAY
(CLOCKWISE)

Illus. 7-53. The bit turns clockwise, so if you move the router counterclockwise around your work, the two forces work against each other to give you control.

Illus. 7-50. Some pieces can be held in a vise for routing as long as they are thick enough. Reposition them if necessary to keep the bit from hitting the vise.

Illus. 7-51. A router mat will hold some pieces securely.

You must keep the router moving at all times when it is touching the wood. If you stop in one place or go too slowly, the bit will burn the wood surface. If you can't do the silhouette in one continuous pass, move the router away from the work before you stop your forward motion. Then overlap your next pass (Illus. 7-54).

OVERLAPPING PASSES

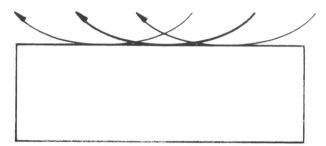

Illus. 7-54. Remove the router from the edge of your work before you stop moving it. Then overlap the next pass and, again, pull it away from your work before you stop moving it.

The hardest areas to rout are tight outside curves, where you have to keep the bit pressed against your work as you change directions (Illus. 7-55). This is where you tend to slow down and burn the edge. Anticipate the curve and try to maintain the router speed as you change directions.

A ¼-inch quarter-round can be routed in one pass, but if you are relatively new to routing, do the job in two or three passes. Set the bit partway out, make a pass, set it out farther, make a pass, set it all the way out, and make your final pass.

Remember, if you are not experienced with the router, you can round the edges by hand with the four-in-hand. Also, the router simply can't reach some areas, so use the four-in-hand to round these areas.

Hand-Sanding

An efficient toymaker will minimize hand-sanding, but there is some hand-sanding that is necessary. This sanding is generally done on the corner between the flat surface (sanded by the wide belt sander) and the edges or silhouette (sanded by the edge sander). On small toy parts, this edge is usually a square corner. This sharp corner will have to be broken, to soften it. On larger parts, these corners are rounded over with a rasp and file or a router. Hand-sanding will remove any roughness left by the file or any burns or roughness left by the router.

When sanding flat surfaces you sand with the grain, but when hand-sanding edges, it is best to sand across the grain. The paper should cut at a 45-degree angle to the edge itself (Illus 7-56). You'll get the most out of your sandpaper sheets if you fold and rip them in quarters (Illus. 7-57). Then fold this piece in half. If you hold the paper between your thumb and pinky, the whole sheet will cut on each pass (Illus. 7-58). You can cut quickly this way and use the whole sheet. When

Illus. 7-55. It is hard to maintain router speed as you change directions around corners. This is where you will tend to burn your work.

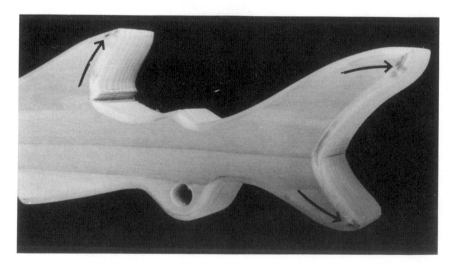

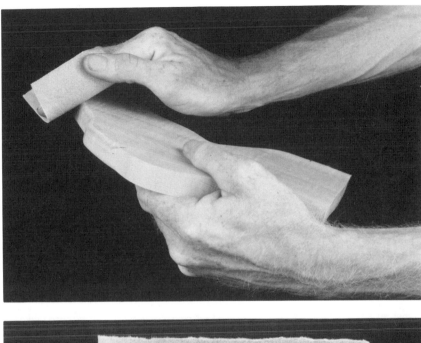

Illus. 7-56. Hold the sandpaper at a 45-degree angle, and sand across the edge.

Illus. 7-57. Fold and rip each sheet in quarters to use it efficiently.

one side is totally worn out, flip it over and continue. Be careful not to hit the flat surface or the silhouette at this point or you will scratch the smooth surfaces.

If you are hand-sanding tight little corners, hold the paper rigid between your fingers and thumb. This will give you a stiff edge to get into those tight spots (Illus. 7-59).

I use #120-grit sandpaper to round the sharp corners of small pieces. For rounded edges, I start with #80-grit sandpaper on rasp marks or router burns, and then switch to #120-grit to finish up. I am a production toymaker, so it is not practical to use finer-grit sandpaper. You can, of course, use finer- and finer-grit sandpapers for a beautiful finish. Don't use a finer sandpaper, though, until you've removed all the scratches from the previous grit.

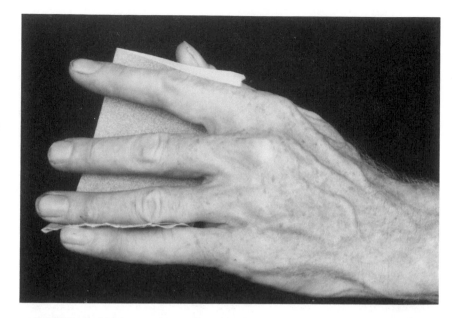

Illus. 7-58. Holding the folded quarter-sheet between your pinky and thumb will give you a wide, well-supported surface. This will enable you to sand quickly and use the entire surface of the paper.

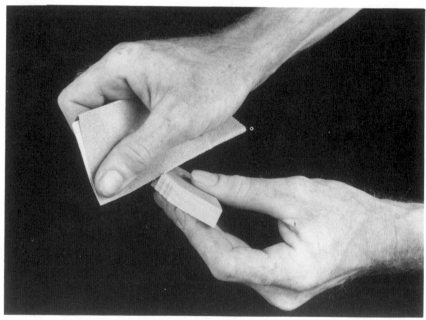

Illus. 7-59. Stretching the piece across your palm will give you a stiff edge for getting into tight corners without rounding off the details.

Dust

Dust is a very serious health hazard. Some dusts, such as walnut, are actually toxic. Also, the small particles of any wood dust can clog the pores of your lungs.

It is essential that you protect yourself from dust inhalation. An inexpensive dust-collection system can be made with a shop vacuum hose that can be attached to individual fittings on each sander when you use them (Illus. 7-60 and 7-61). Make sure to clean the filter regularly or the dust-collection system won't pull the dust.

Anyone planning to become a professional toy-maker should consider setting up a permanent dust-collection system, with one large collector and gates at each fitting, which can be opened (and closed when not in use) (Illus. 7-62 and 7-63).

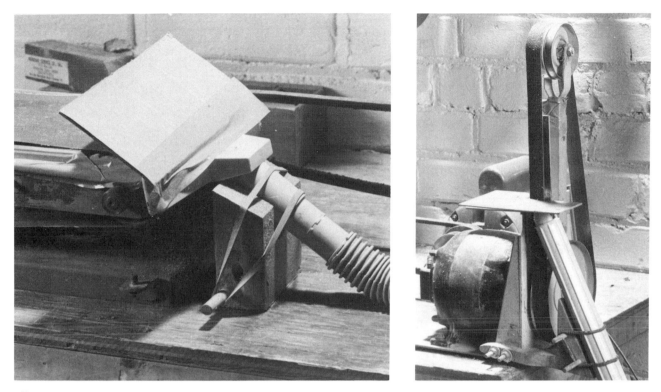

Illus. 7-60 (above left). You can rig up a simple jig to hold a shop vacuum hose in place so it can be used as a dust-collection system for the stationary, wide-belt sander. *Illus. 7-61 (above right).* A simple jig can also be made for the 1-inch edge sander.

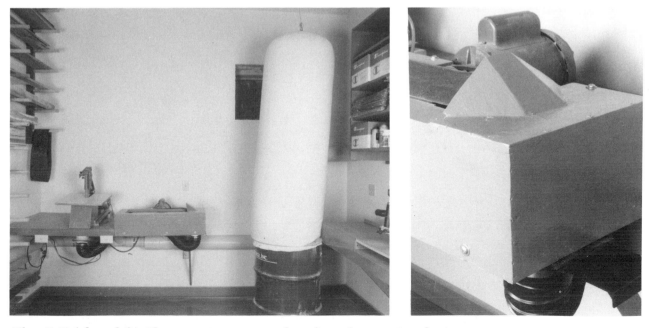

Illus. 7-62 (above left). The more time you spend sanding, the more it makes sense to set up a dust-collection system. *Illus. 7-63 (above right).* A permanent dust-collection system should have a gate at each tool.

Any dust-collection system will remove some but not all dust from the air. A good dust mask is also necessary. A poorly fitted paper mask is ineffective. The dust will go right around it. The mask should fit snugly around your nose and mouth and have replaceable filters. You don't need a vapor mask. They are very expensive, are very heavy, and are hard to breathe through. Use a good-quality sawdust filter mask (Illus. 7-64). Remember that cutting, drilling, and hand-sanding also create sawdust!

Illus. 7-64. A good dust mask should be light and tight-fitting. It should also have replaceable filters.

Chapter 8

ASSEMBLY

The word "assembly" in this chapter has been broadened to include the attachment of at least two pieces. The assembly of toys usually involves gluing and clamping. Below are descriptions of different assembly processes that you will use when making toys.

General Gluing Guidelines

Unlike some glues, aliphatic resin needs to be clamped for about 20–30 minutes as it sets up. Therefore, use C-clamps, bar clamps, or a vise to hold the parts together.

In some cases, to ensure a good joint you will have to apply enough glue so that a little squeezes out. Through practice, you will develop a sense of how much glue is required, without making a mess.

The glue that does squeeze out will have to be removed. If you do this as soon as you've clamped your work, the glue will be pushed into the pores of the wood and will be harder to clean up with sanding. These areas won't absorb oil and will show up in the finishing process (Illus. 8-1). Glue is so strong that if you wait too long, you will tear out little pieces of wood with the glue when you try to scrape it off, and you will certainly "gum up" belts trying to sand it off.

After the glue has dried about 15 minutes, it is the consistency of cottage cheese, and it can be scraped off easily, with a chisel or scraper. Although the glue only needs to be clamped for 20–30 minutes, it has not thoroughly set up at this point. Let the piece set overnight before doing any *serious* work to it, or it may fall apart. Axle ends can be sanded within an hour, though, because this doesn't apply pressure to the glue joint.

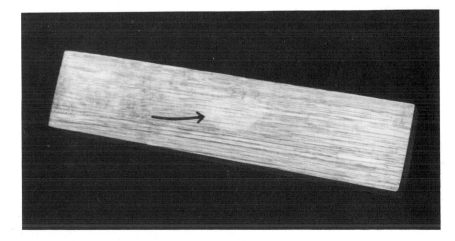

Illus. 8-1. Any glue left on the wood (or pushed into the pores) will prevent that area from absorbing a finish.

Joining Boards on Edge

Quite often you won't be able to find a board wide enough for the toy part you are making. You will have to use more than one board.

Before gluing these boards together, make sure that the edges to be joined are perfectly straight. The jointer is used for this operation. Following are several guidelines for using a jointer:

1. Make sure the in-feed and out-feed tables are parallel. Place a shim under the out-feed table if necessary.

2. The out-feed table should be the same height as the top of the blades.

3. The blades should all be exactly the same height.

4. You should hold the board down on the *out-feed* table after it passes the blades.

5. Joint boards with their concave surfaces down or you will reproduce the same curve over and over again.

When you have jointed the edges to be glued together, you should be able to hold them up and see no light between them. You can clamp boards together that are improperly jointed, but eventually the stresses created will tear the boards apart.

Now that the edges of the boards have been jointed, the next step is to glue the boards to-gether. Lay out your pole clamps with wax paper over them to catch any excess squeeze-out. First, apply a thin layer of glue to one edge and keep the edges lined up with your fingers as you clamp the boards together (Illus 8-2). It's a good idea to put clamps above your work also, to make the pressure uniform and keep the boards parallel (Illus. 8-3). Ideally, there should be a *little* squeeze-out the whole length of the joint. This way, you know there is glue over the entire surfaces and there won't be any visible cracks or weak spots.

If you're gluing up several boards, you'll have to rip the boards and joint the second edges. You may want to clamp a couple of boards (at least 1 inch wide so they stay rigid) above and below your work to keep the assembly flat (Illus. 8-4).

Gluing End Grain

When gluing end grain, you may want to apply glue to both surfaces, because the end grain tends to absorb more glue.

Gluing Flat Surfaces

There are two things to remember when gluing flat surfaces together. First, unless you are sanding the glue joint after assembly, try to avoid any glue squeeze-out. To do this, apply a little less

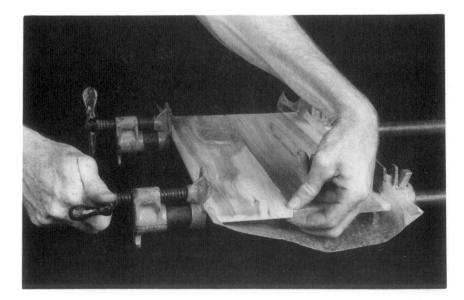

Illus. 8-2. Use your fingertips to line up the ends of the boards as you apply pressure to the clamps.

Illus. 8-3. One way to ensure uniform clamping pressure is to use clamps above and below the glue-up.

Illus. 8-4. A couple of boards clamped above and below the glue-up will keep your work flat. Note the wax paper between the pieces of wood and the glue-up.

glue than usual and work it back from the edges (Illus. 8-5).

Also, be careful as you clamp the pieces. They will have a tendency to move as you apply pressure to the C-clamps. It helps to seat the non-pivoting face of the clamp squarely onto one surface before you tighten the screw to bring the other face against your work (Illus. 8-6).

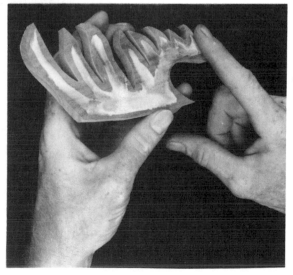

Illus. 8-5 (right). Work the glue away from the edges to avoid squeeze-out.

Illus. 8-6. If the rigid face of the clamp is flush to the work surface, the second clamp face will be flat as it meets the other side. This will prevent shifting as you apply pressure to the clamps.

Gluing Dowels Through Your Work

Quite often, dowels are used for decoration. They can be used for the eyes of animals, etc. When used for such purposes, they will have to be glued all the way through the work.

Put wax paper under your work. Apply a little glue to the *inside* of the hole. If you apply too much glue, it will fill the bottom of the hole and prevent the dowel from going all the way through. If the hole is close to the edge of your work, this excess glue will split the wood apart.

If you put glue on your dowel instead of in the hole, it will all be scraped off onto the surfaces of your work as you drive the dowel home (Illus. 8-7). When you cut your dowel to length, the saw will leave a slight amount of "fuzz" at the end of

Illus. 8-7. If you put the glue on the dowel, instead of in the hole, all the glue will be scraped off as the dowel is hammered into the hole.

the dowel. Round the ends of the dowel with sandpaper before driving it into the hole or this fuzz will grab all the glue and push it out the back of the hole.

Your dowel should be a little longer than the thickness of the wood, so that it protrudes slightly from both sides of the hole. This way, you can sand it flush and produce a smooth, circular surface (Illus. 8-8).

Illus. 8-8. If you make the dowel a little long, it will protrude from both surfaces. This way, you can sand it flush for a clean surface.

When you are hammering the dowel home, it is better to take a few hard swings rather than many small taps. When a few hard swings are used, the dowel is more likely to slide right through (Illus. 8-9). When many small taps are made, the dowel may get stuck, break off, or protrude from the end of the wood.

The dowel is glued into the piece before the piece is cut out. If the dowel protrudes through the underside of the piece, flat-sand the protruding end of the dowel flush to the back side of the piece, so that it will sit flat on the band-saw worktable when you cut it out.

Gluing into Holes with a Sealed End

The procedures for gluing pegs, dowels, or anything else into a hole with a sealed end are much the same as the previous gluing techniques except that you must be even more careful not to apply too much glue in the hole. There is nowhere for the glue to go, so it fills the bottom of the hole and either keeps the part from going into its proper depth or splits the hole open (Illus. 8-10).

If the part that is glued into the hole is under

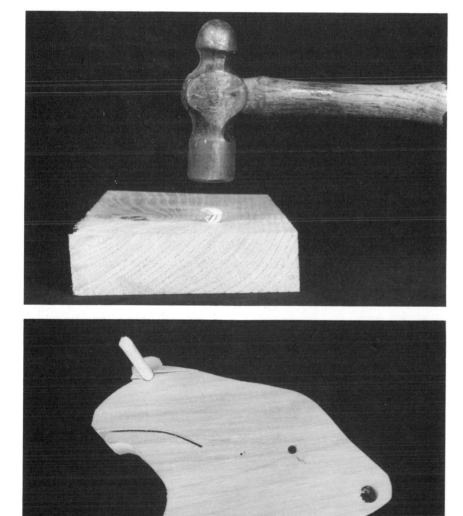

Illus. 8-9. A few hard swings with the hammer will drive the dowel home. If you make a series of light taps, the dowel is likely to protrude from the end of the work or even break off before it is all the way in.

Illus. 8-10. Too much glue in a dead-end hole may end up splitting the wood.

Illus. 8-11. Use a pair of pliers to put a crimp in the end of a dowel. This makes grooves for the glue, which will result in a much stronger joint.

any stress where the part may pull out, crimp or groove its edges to make slots for the glue. This will give the joint much more strength (Illus. 8-11).

Gluing Wheels to Axles

When gluing axles into wheels, crimp glue slots into the axle ends for extra grip. It's also necessary to round the dowel ends with sandpaper to keep the rough edges from pushing all the glue off the sides of the hole. The slightly smaller diameter at the end of the dowel will also make it easier to start the dowel into the wheel hole.

As in the case of *gluing dowels through the work*, make the dowel slightly long (at both ends) so that it protrudes slightly from the wheel's surface. This enables you to sand it back flush to the axle hub or wheel's surface, remove any glue, and smooth the rough axle ends (Illus. 8-12).

Be sure to cut your dowels long enough for clearance between the wheels and the toy. I generally allow 1/16 inch for each pivoting joint; in other words, 1/8 inch total clearance for a set of wheels and an axle (plus slightly extra for the ends to protrude) (Illus. 8-13).

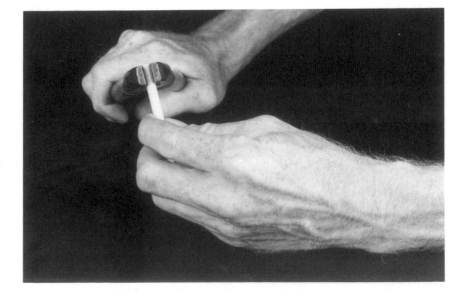

Illus. 8-12. Note that the dowel on the left protrudes from the wheel so that the glue and the rough end of the dowel can be sanded smooth, as shown by the dowel and wheel on the right.

Lay out wax paper on the workbench. Put glue in the axle hole and tap the axle end into the wheel until it protrudes slightly. Again, hard strokes with the hammer work best.

Wipe off the excess glue with a circular, inward sweep of your fingertip, to keep the glue off the rest of the wheel's surface (Illus. 8-14).

Slip the axle through your work and rest the glued wheel flat on the wax paper. Position the second wheel on top of the axle (good side outward) and hammer it on until the axle protrudes slightly. Wipe the excess glue off the axle end (and the hammer face). Tip the wheel slightly to fit it more easily onto the axle (Illus. 8-15).

A piece of old carpet or a rag is handy to wipe off the hammer face between axle glue-ups. This way you won't get glue all over the next wheel.

When you are sanding the axle hubs or wheel surfaces (after the glue has set up), be sure that the grain of the wood lines up with the vertical direction of the sanding belt to avoid cross-grain scratches.

Gluing Outdoor Toys

All of the techniques described in this chapter can be applied to toys that will be left outside. You will, however, have to use a waterproof glue such as Titebond II® because aliphatic resin glues are water-soluble and will break down if they get wet.

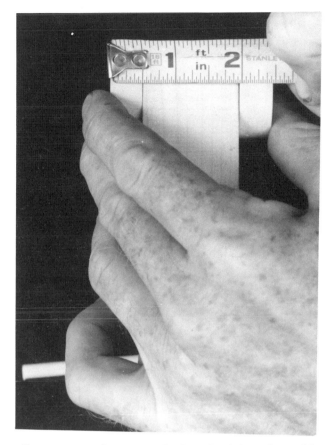

Illus. 8-13. To determine the length of the axles, add the thickness of the toy (1½ inches), the thickness of both wheels (½ inch and ½ inch), the gap allowance on each side of the toy (⅟₁₆ inch and ⅟₁₆ inch), and slightly extra length for protruding axle ends (⅟₁₆ inch), for a total length, in this case, of 2¹¹⁄₁₆ inches.

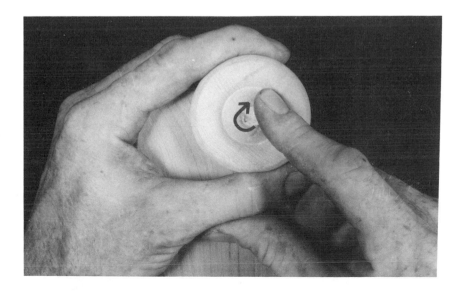

Illus. 8-14. Sweep your fingertip around in an inward circle to remove any excess glue without smearing it all over the wheel.

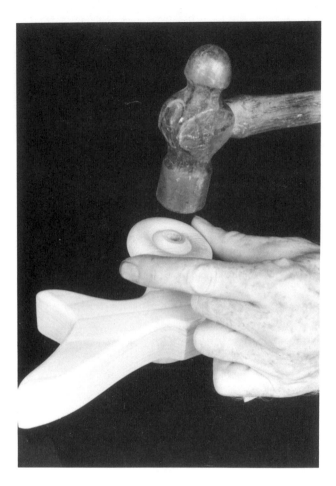

Illus. 8-15. Tip the wheel slightly to fit onto the end of the axle.

Chapter 9
APPLYING A FINISH

A finish is applied to toys for several reasons. It will give the toy some protection from abrasion (scratches, dents, and gouges, etc.). It will protect the toy from dirt and other discolorations that detract from its appearance. Most finishes will keep the wood from absorbing water, to a certain extent (water can, of course, warp and crack a toy). Last, but equally important, a finish will make a toy look better. A clear finish will bring out the grain and depth of color of the wood. A stain (under a clear finish) or a painted finish will give the toy a bright, cheerful appearance.

Bear in mind that some toys can be finished more easily (and thoroughly) before the toy is assembled. Below are descriptions of the different types of finish that can be used on toys.

Penetrating Oils

Mineral and resin oil are both penetrating oils. Mineral oil does not dry. It simply penetrates and maintains its original makeup. This means that it will evaporate over time, so a toy with a mineral-oil finish will eventually have to be refinished. Resin oils such as Watco® Danish Oil Finish and Behlen's® Salad Bowl Oil Finish will soak into the oil and polymerize (harden and dry) under the surface. Toys with these types of finish will not have to be refinished.

The process for applying mineral and resin oils is the same. The toys are dipped in the solution or the finish is wiped on the toys with a rag. Any excess oil is eventually wiped off.

Illus. 9-1. A trough will let the excess oil run back into a bucket. This will conserve oil and make less of a mess.

When you are working with resin oils, wear rubber gloves while handling the toys until they dry. Resin oil is toxic until it sets up thoroughly. Also, make sure that there is adequate ventilation where you are working.

If you decide to dip the toys into the solution, a trough will be helpful. You can set the toys in the trough and let the excess oil run back into a five-gallon bucket. This will save a lot of finish and make the job neater. There is a little block on the underside of the bottom of the trough shown in Illus. 9-1 to keep it from sliding into the bucket.

Although the angle of the trough will depend on the toys you're making, angles of 35–40 degrees seem to work fine. If the angles are any steeper, the toys will slide into the bucket. If the angles are any shallower, the excess oil doesn't run into the bucket quickly enough. The thickness of the toy and the smoothness of the surface will determine whether the toy has to be dipped more than once.

Dip your gloves in the finish before handling your toys. Some rubber gloves will break down in certain solutions, leaving colored smudges on the toys.

Clear, Hard Finishes

Never put a clear, hard finish on any infant toy. These finishes are generally toxic if swallowed, and infants put everything in their mouths. However, many toys for older children will look great with a clear, hard finish. It will give them excellent protection from water, dirt, and abrasion.

Be sure to maintain adequate ventilation when applying hard finishes. Sand lightly but thoroughly between coats. If the toy is going to be used outside, don't forget the hard-to-reach places where water will collect and rot the wood. This happens frequently inside pivot holes (Illus. 9-2). Remember that end grain will absorb more finish and will usually require *at least* one more coat than other surfaces (Illus. 9-3). Apply four or five coats (and more on end grain) to toys that will be used outside. Toys take so much abuse that the finish will wear off.

Stains and Dyes

Experiment on wood before applying stains or dye to toys you've spent many hours making. Determine the following:

Will the stain rub off on a child's clothes or skin? Is the stain *non-toxic*? Is the stain compatible with the hard finish you're going to apply over it? Will the stain dissolve if it gets wet and make a mess?

Illus. 9-2. Don't forget those hard-to-reach spots where water will collect.

Illus. 9-3. End grain will absorb more finish and will require at least one more coat than the other surfaces.

Paint

Enamel paint is recommended for toys because it holds up very well to weather and rough play. But whatever paint you decide on, be sure to apply a good primer coat first, and sand lightly but thoroughly between coats.

As with clear, hard finishes, the end grain will soak up more paint and will probably require an extra coat. Again, don't forget to paint those hard-to-reach areas where water will collect and rot your wood.

Chapter 10
PROJECTS

I have designed these projects with definite goals in mind. I have included toys from several areas of toymaking as an introduction to most types of toys that you will want to make. I've also tried to include toys for children who range in age from infancy (the rattle) to the beginning of adolescence (the swing). Last (and most important), I have tried to include as many tools and techniques as possible.

If the types of toy shown here intrigue you, you may be interested in my other books, which are primarily design books: *How to Make Animated Toys* and *Making Dinosaur Toys in Wood*. Both books are available from Sterling Publishing Co., Inc., 387 Park Avenue South, New York, New York 10016.

Infant Rattle

The infant rattle is a good project on which to practise drilling accuracy and using a four-in-hand. The end result is a very sleek rattle that is pleasing to an infant's eyes, ears, and fingers (Illus. 10-1).

To make an infant rattle, first choose a hardwood like maple, beech, or cherry that's not likely to splinter when it's chewed on. Then do the following:

1. Cut out a blank that's $1\frac{3}{4} \times 1\frac{3}{4} \times 6$ inches and crosscut it into three pieces, leaving the ends a little long.

2. Locate and drill the holes to their proper depth. Use a center punch and a Forstner or bradpoint bit for accuracy.

3. Cut the 1-inch dowels to their proper lengths, round off their ends with sandpaper, and glue the dowels into either side of the central piece.

4. Fill the rattle with beebees. Don't fill the hole more than halfway or the beebees won't have enough room to move and make noise.

5. Glue the dowels to the piece. Usually, glue is put into the hole rather than on the dowel, but in

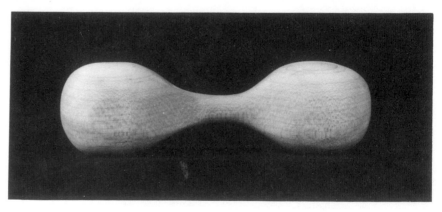

Illus. 10-1. Infant's rattle.

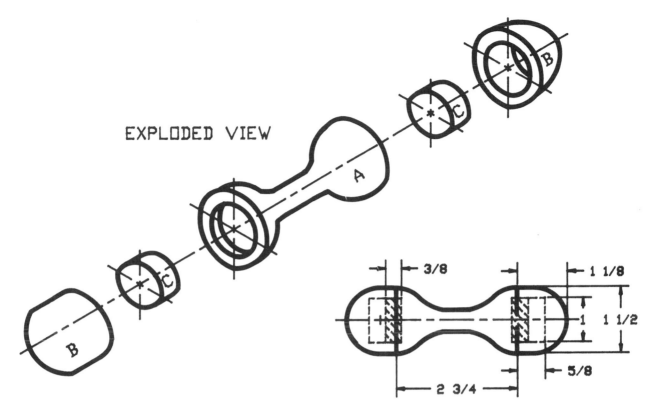

EXPLODED VIEW

FRONT AND TOP VIEWS

Illus. 10-2. Exploded view of infant's rattle.

Part Letter	Part Description	Quantity	Thickness	Width or Diameter	Length
A	Center	1	1½″	1½″	2¾″
B	End	2	1½″	1½″	1⅛″
C	Joining Plugs	2		1″	⅜″
D	BB's				

Parts list for the infant's rattle.

this case put the glue on the outside of the dowel to prevent the glue from being pushed into the rattle's cavity. Put glue on the flat surface of the central piece as well, so all the surfaces will be glued.

6. Line the grain up from piece to piece as you tap the central piece into the rattle end.

7. Repeat step six for the other end and clamp the assembly.

8. When the glue has set up, sand the piece lightly with a belt sander. This removes glue squeeze-out, so the piece will sit flat on the band-saw table when you cut it out.

9. Lay the pattern out on two consecutive sides

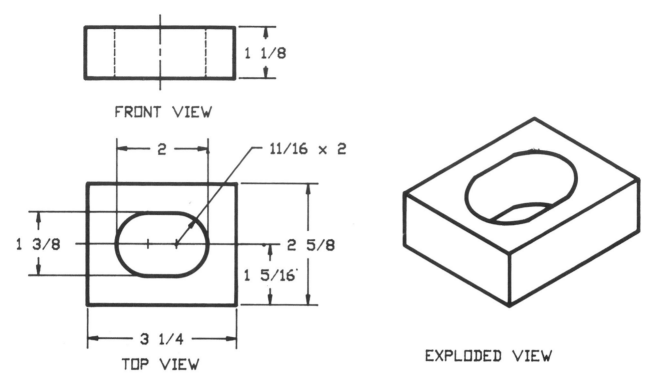

FRONT VIEW

TOP VIEW

EXPLODED VIEW

Illus. 10-3. If you want to design an infant's toy, you should make the block shown here. The government has determined that a safe infant's toy may not extend through this hole or slip through it. Theoretically, this hole represents an infant's mouth and the toy must be large enough not to be swallowed or choke an infant.

and cut it out. When you cut out the silhouette, leave a little wood at the ends and at the "waist" to hold the scraps on (Illus. 10-4). This will allow you to see the pattern on the second side when you flip the piece on the next edge.

10. Cut out the second silhouette all the way around.

11. Go back to the first silhouette and finish cutting the scrap away from it.

12. Edge-sand both silhouettes. Be careful not to remove too much wood from the "waist" area.

13. Round the corners. If you're good with an

edge sander, you can take a lot of the excess material off the corners before you start the hand work. Otherwise, start right in with the four-in-hand. Thoroughly round all the edges with the four-in-hand, starting with the rasp and smoothing with the file.

14. Hand-sand with #80-, #120-, and #150-grit paper. Don't move from one grit to the next until all the scratches have been removed. You may want to go to finer sandpaper for an extremely smooth finish.

Illus. 10-4. When cutting out the silhouette, leave some wood at the ends and at the "waist" to hold the scraps on.

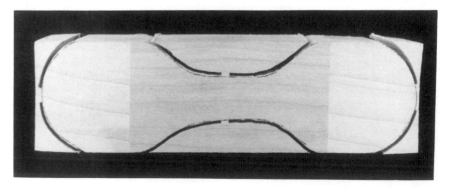

15. Add a finish. Non-toxic dyes can make the rattle bright and cheerful. If using a non-toxic dye, next apply a non-toxic oil finish. Note the drying times for the oil that you use. For example, Watco Oil must dry for 30 days to thoroughly set up and become non-toxic.

Building Blocks

Building blocks are about the most versatile toy you can make (Illus. 10-5). Children start playing with them at an early age and will continue enjoying them until they are seven or eight. They are virtually indestructible and will last for generations. They're also a great toy because they encourage children to use their imagination.

You can make your blocks out of hardwood or softwood. Softwood blocks can be made out of building scraps. They are light. Hardwood toys are heavier, which makes them a little more pleasing to play with. They also won't dent as easily and can be quite attractive if you use wood like cherry or walnut or even a combination of woods. The pillars are made out of 1½-inch closet rod, available at lumberyards. (One-and-one-quarter-inch closet rod will work, too.)

The most important thing in making building blocks is being sure that the dimensions are uniform. For example, if the blocks are 1½ inch thick, two blocks on top of each other should be 3 inches. Note from Illus. 10-6–10-8 that all of these blocks are in increments of 1½ and 3 inches. They are sized for softwood scraps (2 × 4s, etc.), which will be 1½ inch thick.

If you use hardwood, either plane your wood down to 1½ inches or use it at 1¾ inches and change all the sizes to accommodate that thickness. If you choose to do the latter, blocks 3 × 6 inches will become 3½ × 7 inches. The ¾-inch-thick planks will have to be ⅞ inch. When you have enlarged the arches, door, and buttress patterns to 100 percent, enlarge them once more at 116 percent and they will be almost perfectly sized.

To make the building blocks, do the following:

1. Make the blocks. You can use a table saw for some of the blocks and to make blocks for the wedges and triangles, etc., that will be split in half on the band saw. Another approach is to cut all of the blocks out on the band saw. Make sure that you hold the dowels firmly as you crosscut the pillars to length. The blade tends to grab them and tries to yank them down and forward. You will have to glue up a blank for the Gothic arch.

You may want to cut the blocks *slightly* oversize to account for the material that will be removed with the belt sander.

2. Sand all the surfaces with a belt sander and an edge sander.

3. Round all the edges except the sharp ends of the wedges and triangles. These edges can be broken slightly with a file and sandpaper. If the edges are too sharp they may hurt someone, and

Illus. 10-5. Building blocks.

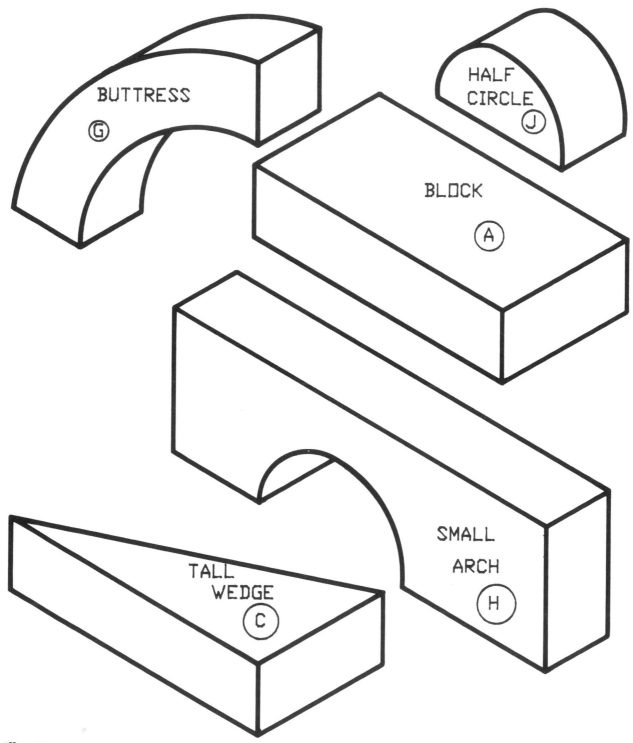

Illus. 10-6–10-8. *Isometric view of the building blocks. See page 112 for the parts list.*

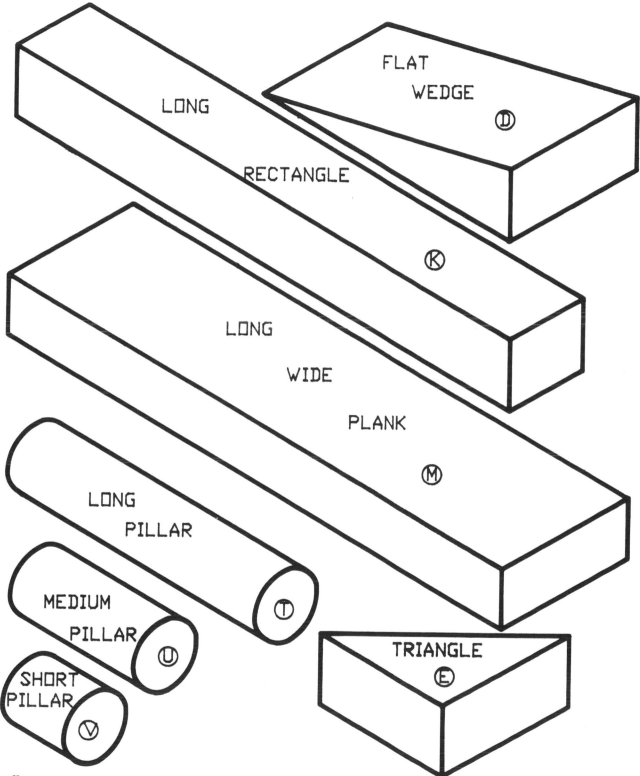

Illus. 10-7.

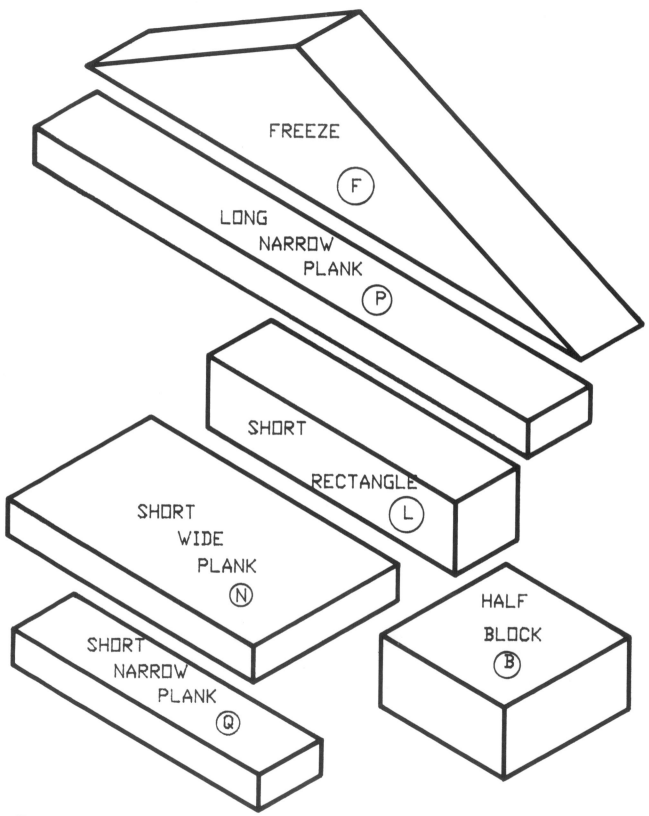

FREEZE
F

LONG
NARROW
PLANK
P

SHORT

RECTANGLE
L

SHORT
WIDE
PLANK
N

SHORT
NARROW
PLANK
Q

HALF
BLOCK
B

Illus. 10-8.

SCALE: FULL SIZE

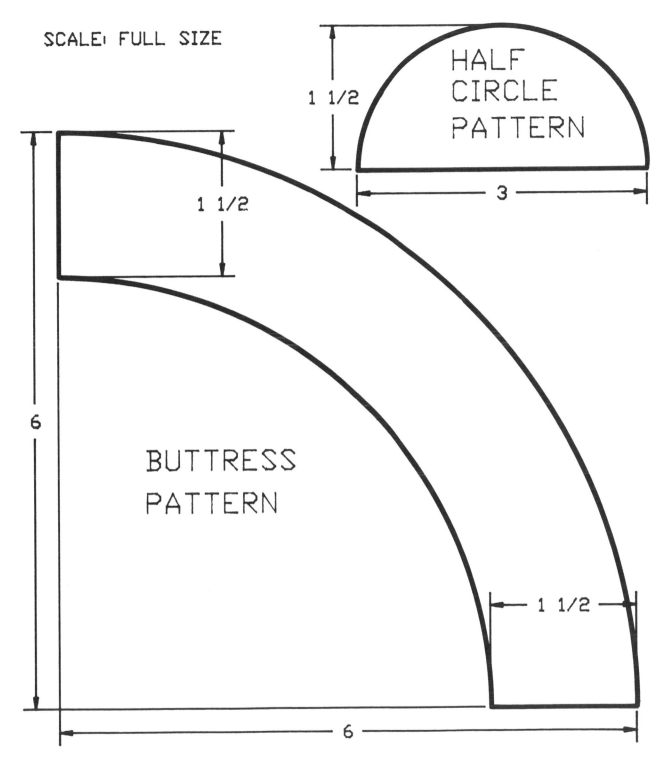

HALF
CIRCLE
PATTERN

1 1/2

3

1 1/2

6

BUTTRESS
PATTERN

1 1/2

6

Illus. 10-9. Buttress pattern.

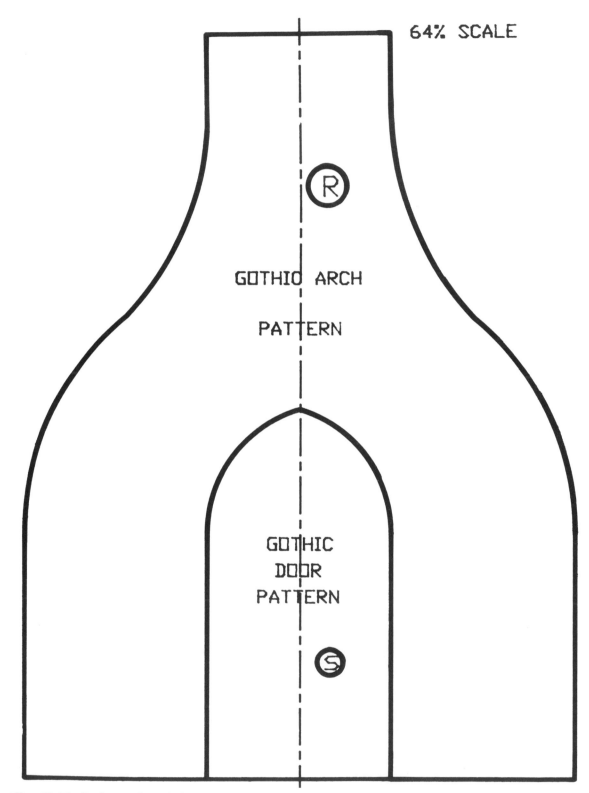

64% SCALE

GOTHIC ARCH

PATTERN

GOTHIC
DOOR
PATTERN

Illus. 10-10. Gothic arch and door pattern. It is at 64 percent of its original size. To get it to 100 percent, photocopy this pattern at 125 percent, and photocopy the resulting photocopy at 125 percent.

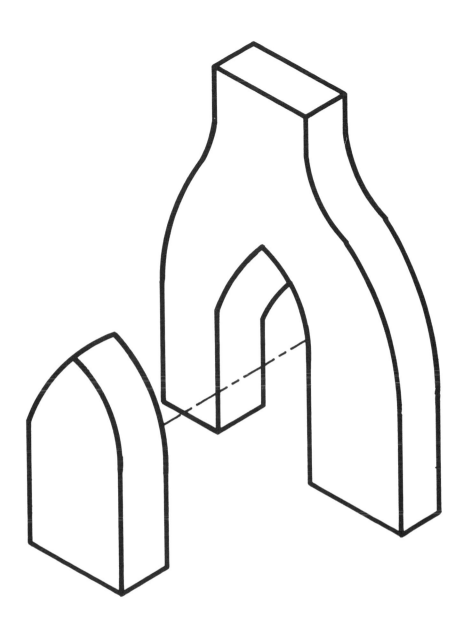

Illus. 10-11. An exploded view of the Gothic door and arch pattern.

they'll also chip easily. However, the sharper the points, the more smoothly toy cars, etc., will roll onto the ramp. Bevel the ends of the pillars on the edge sander or by hand.

4. Hand-sand all the rounded edges, etc. The smoother the blocks are, the more pleasing they are to handle and play with.

5. Apply a non-toxic finish. Bright-colored dyes (again, non-toxic) can be an interesting touch.

Part Letter	Part Description	Quantity	Thickness	Width or Diameter	Length
A	Block	8	1½″	3″	6″
B	Half Block	8	1½″	3″	3″
C	Tall Wedge	4	1½″	3″	6″
D	Flat Wedge	4	1½″	3″	6″
E	Triangle	4	1½″	3″	3″
F	Freeze	2	1½″	3″	12″
G	Buttress	2	1½″	6″	6″
H	Small Arch	1	1½″	3″	9″
J	Half Circle	1	1½″	1½″	3″
K	Long Rectangle	2	1½″	1½″	12″
L	Short Rectangle	2	1½″	1½″	6″
M	Long Wide Plank	2	¾″	3″	12″
N	Short Wide Plank	2	¾″	3″	6″
P	Long Narrow Plank	2	¾″	1½″	12″
Q	Short Narrow Plank	2	¾″	1½″	6″
R	Gothic Arch	1	1½″	9″	12″
S	Gothic Door	1	1½″	3″	6″
T	Long Pillar	4		1½″	6″
U	Medium Pillar	4		1½″	3″
V	Short Pillar	4		1½″	1½″

Parts list for the building blocks.

The Palette Puzzle

There are many types of jigsaw puzzles, but the type best suited for small children has totally enclosed single pieces (Illus. 10-12). These puzzles help children to develop their sense of shape, size, and spatial relationships. This particular puzzle has the added advantage of helping them to learn different colors as they start to become familiar with the alphabet and simple sounds. The little handles make it easy to fit pieces in and out of the puzzle.

Plywood works well for jigsaw puzzles because it doesn't warp. Its main advantage, though, is that the grain in the separate plies goes in opposite directions, so the pieces won't break along the grain.

To make the jigsaw puzzle, do the following:

1. Lay out the pattern on a piece of ⅜-inch-thick plywood.

2. Drill a hole the size of the scroll-saw blade somewhere on the silhouette of each piece.

3. Insert the scroll-saw blade through the holes one at a time and carefully cut out each piece. This can be done with a coping saw as well by clamping

the piece in a vise (or at least to a tabletop) as you cut the pieces out.

4. Drill a ⅜-inch hole in the center of each piece and glue a ¾-inch-long piece of ⅜-inch dowel in each hole. (Be sure to hold the dowel firmly if you use a band saw to crosscut the pieces. The blade will tend to grab the dowel.)

5. When the glue has dried, sand the bottom of the pieces flat on the belt sander to smooth off the glue.

6. Hand-sand all the edges of the pieces, the handles, and the silhouettes.

7. Lay out the pattern on a ¼-inch-thick piece of plywood that will serve as the backing.

8. Glue and clamp the silhouette to the backing. Be careful to work glue away from the edges

of the silhouettes before joining the two pieces, to avoid squeeze-out.

9. First, use the 1-inch sander-grinder on the outer edges of the puzzle and then hand-sand them. Use Lettraset to label the holes for their respective colors.

10. Put a clear finish over the entire puzzle base to protect the lettering. Stain the puzzle pieces with non-toxic dyes and coat them too, if desired. Or paint the pieces instead, with non-toxic latex paint.

You can make up endless varieties of this type of puzzle. Anything you can imagine can be glued to the top of the puzzle with spray adhesive and cut out for puzzle pieces.

Illus. 10-12. Palette puzzle.

Part Letter	Part Description	Quantity	Thickness	Width or Diameter	Length
A	Puzzle and Pieces	1	⅜″	7½″	10¾″
B	Backing	1	¼″	7½″	10¾″
C	Handles	7		⅜″	¾″

Parts list for the palette puzzle.

80% X 125% = 100%

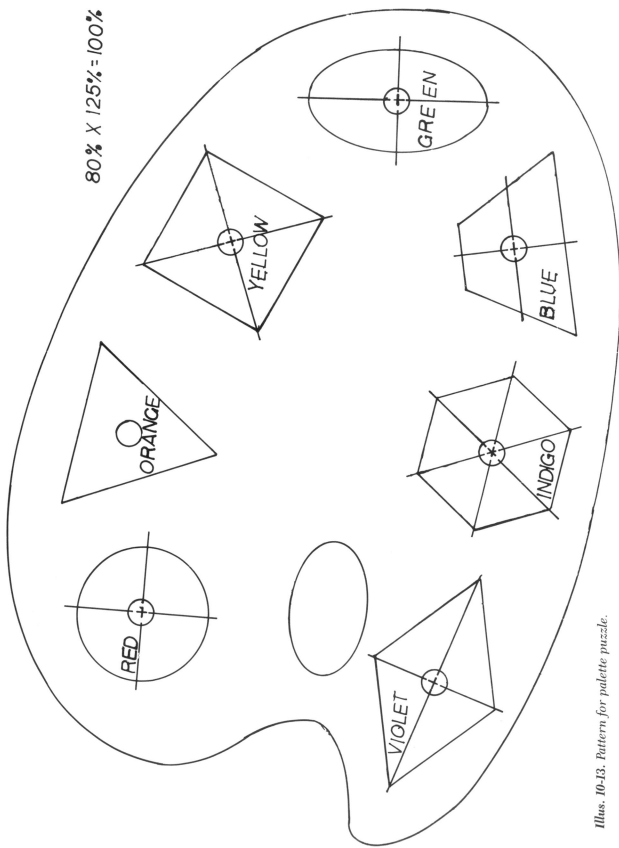

GREEN

YELLOW

BLUE

ORANGE

INDIGO

RED

VIOLET

Illus. 10-13. Pattern for palette puzzle.

Shark

The jaws on this animated push toy open menacingly and then chomp down with a dreadful finality (Illus. 10-14). As the shark is pushed along, the dowels inside the front wheels push the back of the jaw down, which lifts up the snout (pivoting on the eye peg).

Body

Lay out the body. Drill the holes accurately, and then cut out the silhouette. Sand the body flat and then sand and rout all the edges except the teeth and the slot for the fins. Break the edges on the teeth with a file to keep the line crisp. Sand all the routed edges, etc., by hand.

Fin

Lay out the fin. Cut it out, sand it flat, and then sand the edges. Break the edges by hand with sandpaper and set the fin aside for final assembly.

Head

Lay out the head spacer and cut it out. Don't sand the sides flat or they may end up not being parallel, and that will interfere with the head's smooth movement after assembly.

Lay out the head sides, drill the eye holes *accurately*, and cut them out *carefully*. The success of the toy relies on the accuracy of the head assembly. Sand the head sides flat and the edges of the teeth and the bottom of rear edges (not where the spacer will be glued; this edge is sanded after assembly). Be careful not to remove too much material from the lower rear edge where the dowel will push to lift the head.

A simple jig will help to line the head sides up perfectly during assembly. Drill a ¼-inch hole into a block of wood and glue and tap a ¼-inch dowel into it (Illus. 10-18). Slip both head sides onto the jig and glue and clamp them to the spacer (Illus. 10-19). When the glue has set up, sand the snout edge of the assembly where the sides meet the spacer. Then break all the edges by hand with sandpaper. Use a file to break the edges of the teeth.

Wheels and Dowels

Drill the ½-inch holes inside the front wheels. When you glue the dowels into the front wheels, be sure that they are perpendicular to the wheels' surface (Illus. 10-20). Cut the axles to length and slightly round the ends.

Assembly

If you're going to paint your shark, now is the time to do it, before assembly. It can be oiled after assembly. Now, attach the head to the body with

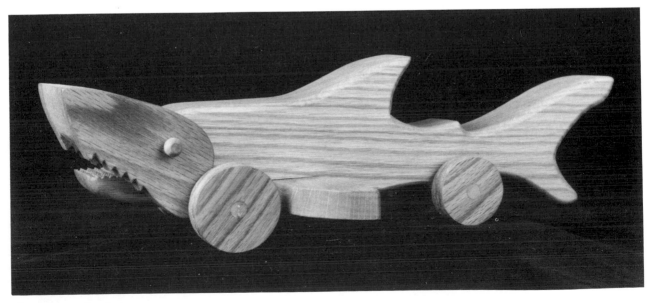

Illus. 10-14. Shark.

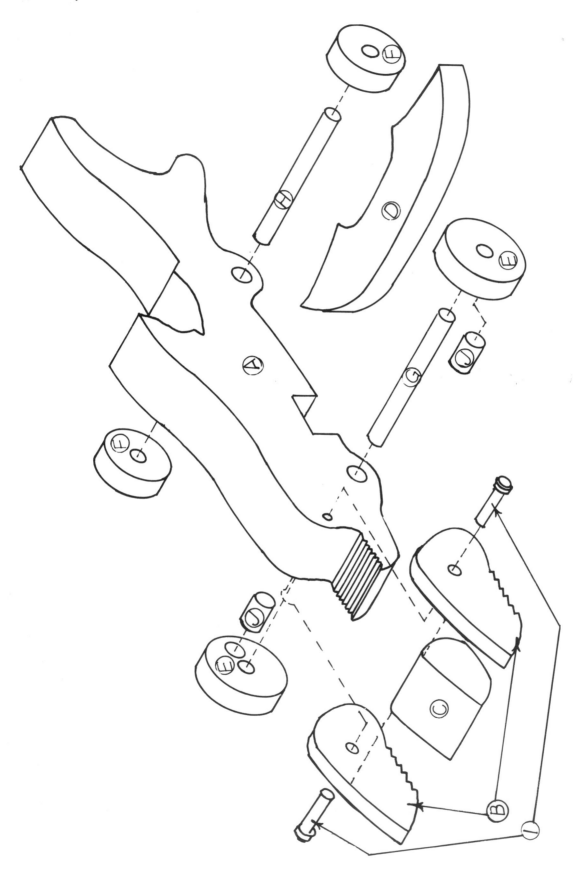

Illus. 10-15. Exploded view of shark.

SHARK PATTERNS

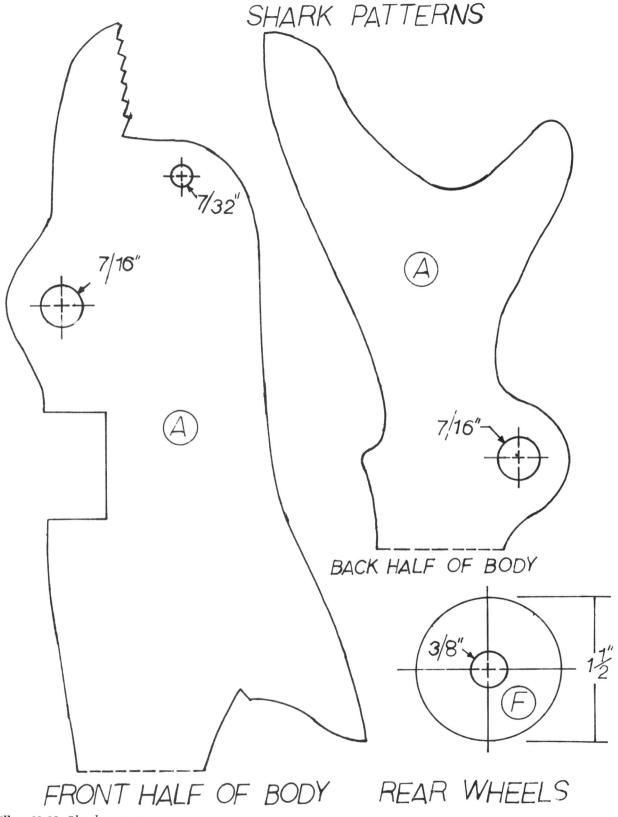

7/32"

7/16"

Ⓐ

Ⓐ

BACK HALF OF BODY

7/16"

3/8"

1½"

Ⓕ

FRONT HALF OF BODY　　REAR WHEELS

Illus. 10-16. Shark patterns.

SHARK PATTERN

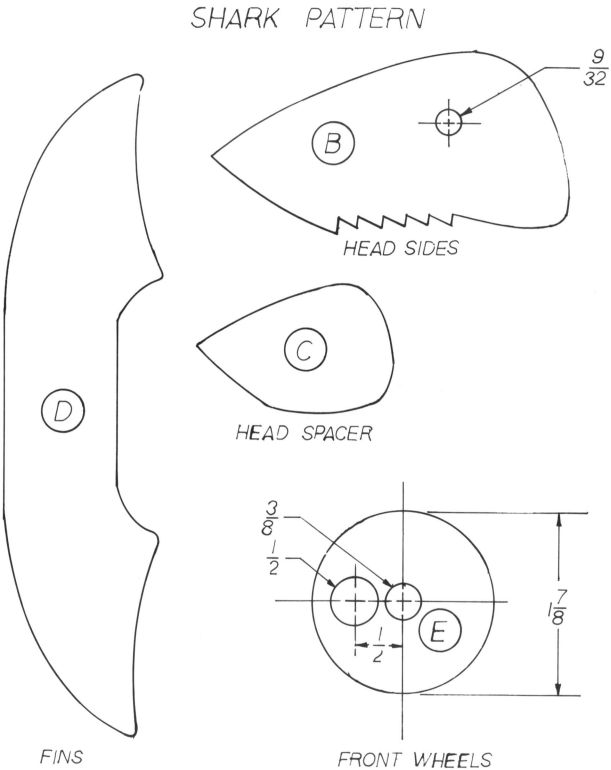

HEAD SIDES

HEAD SPACER

FINS

FRONT WHEELS

Illus. 10-17. Shark patterns.

Part Letter	Part Description	Quantity	Thickness	Width or Diameter	Length
A	Body	1	1½″	3¾″	13¼″
B	Head Sides	2	½″	1⅞″	3¾″
C	Head Spacer	1	1⅝″	1⅜″	2″
D	Fins	1	⅝″	1⅝″	6⅞″
E	Front Wheels	2	½″	1⅞″	
F	Rear Wheels	2	½″	1½″	
G	Front Axle	1		⅜″	3⅜″
H	Rear Axle	1		⅜″	2⅝″
J	Wheel Plugs	2		½″	¾″
K	Pegs	2		⁷⁄₃₂″	1¹⁄₁₆″ shaft

Parts list for shark.

Illus. 10-18. *A simple jig for assembling the head can be made by drilling a ¼-inch hole at a right angle to a block of wood and gluing a ¼-inch dowel in the hole.*

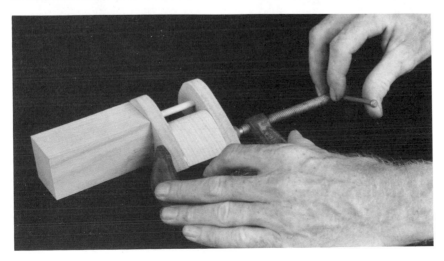

Illus. 10-19. *The jig will help to line up the sides of the head during assembly.*

Illus. 10-20. Make sure that the dowels inside the wheels are perpendicular to the wheels' surface.

NO   NO   YES

two pegs, without any glue. Check the head's movement and remove wood around the eye holes in the body piece, if necessary. Next, attach the head to the body with pegs and glue. Make sure that the head is centered with 1/16-inch clearance of the peg heads on either side.

Glue the rear wheels on. Twist the front wheels on (without glue) just far enough to check movement on one side and then the other. If something is off, you may be able to fix it by sawing off the dowels inside the front wheels and drilling new holes, etc.

If everything looks good, then glue the front wheels on with one dowel up and one dowel down. Be sure to leave enough clearance for smooth movement. When the glue has dried, sand the axle ends.

With the shark upside down, position the fins and drill the hole for the screw. Then glue and screw the fin in place.

When the glue has set up thoroughly, apply the oil finish. You now have a "Land Shark."

Horse Glider

This classic glider can be hung inside or out (Illus. 10-21). It's a great toy to have in the basement or on the porch, where children can swing for hours even on rainy days. Keep in mind it needs three points to hang from, unlike a conventional swing, so a regular swing set will not accept it without alterations.

If you're going to hang the horse glider outside (from a tree), you can make it out of weather-resistant woods such as cedar, white oak, catalpa, black locust, or osage orange.

Illus. 10-21. Horse glider.

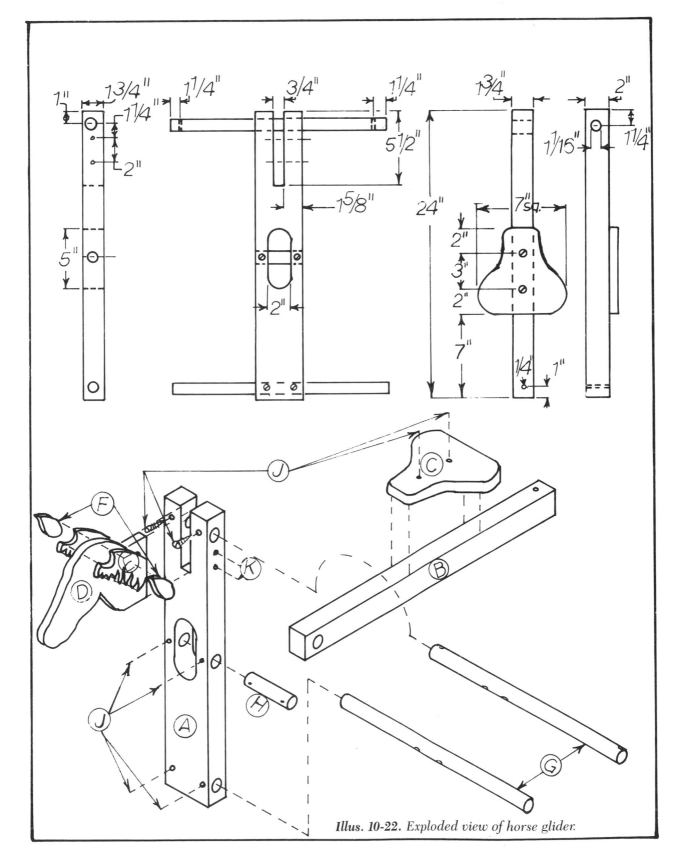

Illus. 10-22. Exploded view of horse glider.

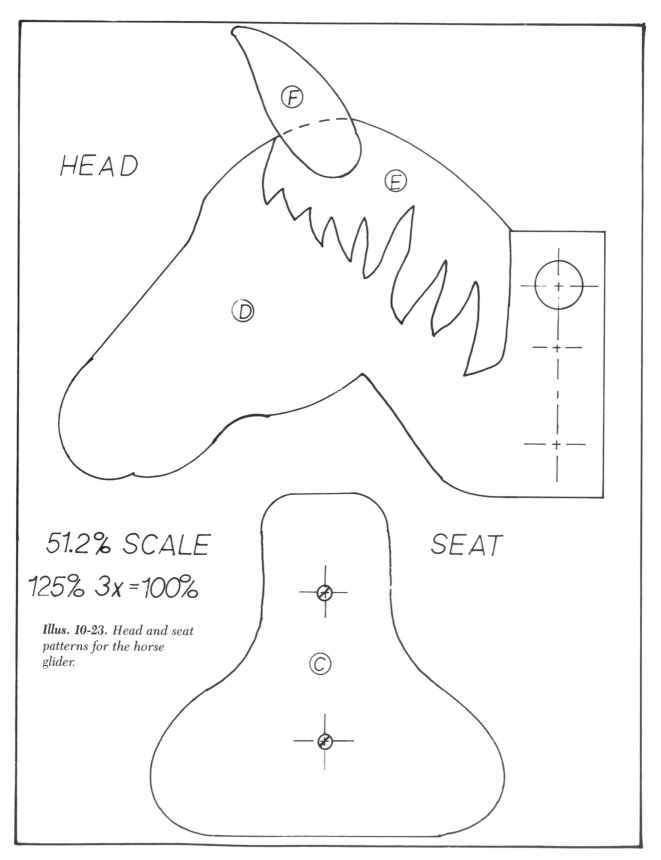

HEAD

F

E

D

51.2% SCALE
125% 3x =100%

SEAT

C

Illus. 10-23. *Head and seat patterns for the horse glider.*

Part Letter	Part Description	Quantity	Thickness	Width or Diameter	Length
A	Vertical Piece	1	1¾″	4″	24″
B	Horizontal Piece	1	1¾″	2″	24″
C	Seat	1	¾″	7″	7″
D	Head	1	¾″	7¾″	10⅞″
E	Mane	2	½″	2⅞″	6¼″
F	Ears	2	½″	1⁷⁄₁₆″	3¾″
G	Handle and Foot Bars	2		1″	18″
H	Pivot Dowel	1		1″	4″
J	Screws (stainless steel or brass for outdoors)	8		#8	1¼″
K	Screws (stainless steel or brass for outdoors)	2		#8	3″

Parts list for horse glider.

You can also treat the swing with mineral-spirit-based stain, paint it, or coat it with polyurethane. Unless you can turn handlebars out of one of the rot-resistant woods, you'll have to make them out of 1-inch maple or birch dowels and stain, paint, or polyurethane them. For an indoor glider, use any strong hardwood.

Head

Cut out the head, sand it flat, and sand and rout the edges, except where the mane will be attached and where the back of the head will be flush to the vertical piece (Illus. 10-24). Cut out the ears and the mane pieces and fit the ears to the gullets in the mane where they will be set. Sand all the pieces and glue the mane pieces to the head. Make sure that the mane will not prevent the head from fitting into the slot in the vertical piece. Sand the edges on the top of the neck and mane after the glue has dried. Rout these edges and glue the ears in place.

Vertical Piece

Cut out the 1¾ × 4 × 24-inch blank and drill the

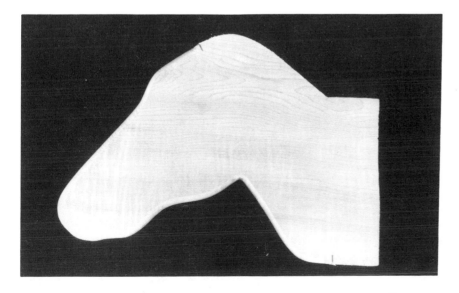

Illus. 10-24. The head on the horse glider. Note that the routing stops where the mane and the vertical piece will be attached to the head.

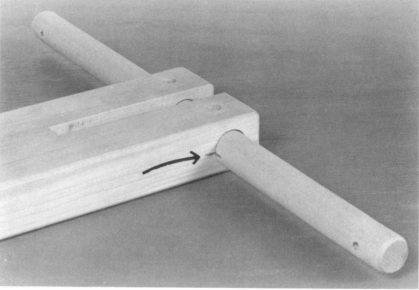

Illus. 10-25. A simple mark will help you line up the handlebar screw holes when you reinsert the handlebar after attaching the head.

three holes. Remove the material from the pivot area by drilling holes and using the jigsaw. Sand all the surfaces and rout all of the edges. Then cut out the ¾ × 5½-inch slot, using the thickness of the head to determine the actual width of the slot.

Horizontal Piece

Cut out the 1¾ × 2 × 24-inch blank and drill the 1¹⁄₁₆-inch hole in one end and the ¼-inch hole in the other. (Make sure that the 1¹⁄₁₆-inch hole goes through the 2-inch-wide surface and the ¼-inch hole goes through the 1¾-inch surface.) Sand all the surfaces and rout the edges.

Cut out and sand the seat and glue and screw it to the horizontal piece.

Dowels

Cut the three dowels to length. Drill the ¼-inch holes in the handlebars. Rout the ends of the handlebars and foot bars by clamping them in a vertical position and moving the router around them counterclockwise, resting it on the ends.

Assembly

Tap the handlebars into place, making sure that the ¼-inch holes will be vertical. Drill the screw holes. Use a pencil to mark the position where the handlebar meets the side of the vertical piece (Illus. 10-26). Tap the handlebar out again.

Position the head in the slot and drill the 1-inch hole through the head. Then drill and screw the head in place with the two 3-inch screws.

Tap the handlebar back into position and screw it into place. Then position the foot bar and the 4-inch pivot dowel and drill the screw holes to secure them. Screw the foot bar into place and mark the position of the pivot dowel as you did the handlebar. Tap the pivot dowel out. If you're going to paint or apply polyurethane to your glider, coat the inside of the 1¹⁄₁₆-inch hole in the horizontal piece and the pivot dowel itself before assembly. Then position the horizontal and vertical pieces (seat up) and tap the pivot dowel through both of them so that your pencil marks line up on the pivot dowel and the side of the horizontal piece. Screw the pivot dowel in place. The glider is complete.

Hanging the Glider

To hang the swing from a ceiling, simply drill ¼-inch holes into the joists and screw in 1-inch eye screws. Make sure that the ropes will be vertical (Illus. 10-26).

If you are hanging your glider from a tree, a board bolted or screwed between two branches may help to get the proper position for the eye screws. The eye screws should all be at the same height.

If you use S hooks on the upper ends of your ropes, they will reduce wear on the ropes and enable you to take the swing down easily. Use ¼-inch nylon to hang the glider. Wrap it once around the handlebar before tying it off securely. Tape the knots at both ends to make sure they can't work their way loose. Inspect them from time to time and the condition of the rope itself.

HANGING THE GLIDER

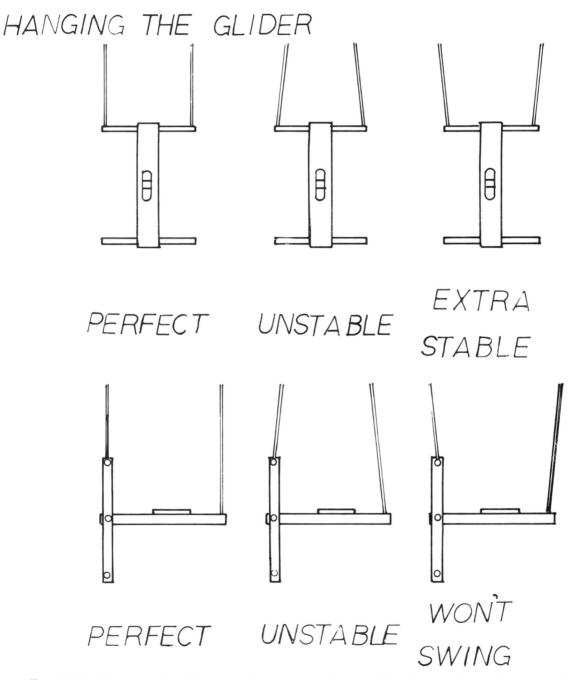

Illus. 10-26. The ropes should hang as close to vertical as possible. This may be tricky if you're hanging a glider from a tree.

Metric Equivalents

INCHES TO MILLIMETRES AND CENTIMETRES

MM—millimetres   CM—centimetres

Inches	MM	CM	Inches	CM	Inches	CM
⅛	3	0.3	9	22.9	30	76.2
¼	6	0.6	10	25.4	31	78.7
⅜	10	1.0	11	27.9	32	81.3
½	13	1.3	12	30.5	33	83.8
⅝	16	1.6	13	33.0	34	86.4
¾	19	1.9	14	35.6	35	88.9
⅞	22	2.2	15	38.1	36	91.4
1	25	2.5	16	40.6	37	94.0
1¼	32	3.2	17	43.2	38	96.5
1½	38	3.8	18	45.7	39	99.1
1¾	44	4.4	19	48.3	40	101.6
2	51	5.1	20	50.8	41	104.1
2½	64	6.4	21	53.3	42	106.7
2	76	7.6	22	55.9	43	109.2
3½	89	8.9	23	58.4	44	111.8
4	102	10.2	24	61.0	45	114.3
4½	114	11.4	25	63.5	46	116.8
5	127	12.7	26	66.0	47	119.4
6	152	15.2	27	68.6	48	121.9
7	178	17.8	28	71.1	49	124.5
8	203	20.3	29	73.7	50	127.0

Index